Who Wants More Death?

Who Wants More Death?

SOCIAL ISSUES IN
CONTEMPORARY AMERICA

● ● ●

Dan Krause

ISBN-13: 9781523957927
ISBN-10: 1523957921

Also by Dan Krause

Contents

CHAPTER 1

Why You Need To Read This Book!

● ● ●

I SHOULD CALL THIS INITIAL chapter "the introduction," but that is not the best way to start a book. Potential readers want to know what a book is about, and they don't want to invest a lot of time finding out. They don't give an author more than a few lines to grab their attention. If he piques their interest, they buy the book. If not, they put it back on the shelf or into the Kindle file, wherever that might be. So my first sentence should be simple and direct: read this book!

For an alternative appeal, there is, of course, the title. But a book title usually doesn't say much about its content. In the old days of libraries, card catalogs, and bookstores, titles meant something. The books some of us grew up with, *The Scarlet Letter, Moby Dick, The Adventures of Tom Sawyer, and The Grapes of Wrath*, a few titles were more obscure than others, but most had a suggestion of what was inside. To contemporary readers, a title like *Moby Dick* conjures up images of the Clarence Thomas confirmation hearings; a generation ago, readers knew it was the name of a whale and that the book was an adventure story.

But book titles are primarily marketing devices now. Titles for both books and movies always have been about marketing, but the situation is different now. It would not be surprising if sales people in today's publishing empires come up with a catchy title first, and then find someone to write a book or screenplay that fits the appealing title. You can never be sure which came first, the horse or the cart. I just finished a "Great Courses" series on publishing, and the instructor warned not to be committed to our titles because the publishers "will almost certainly change them."

As for my title: *Who Favors More Death?*, the content did come first. But after devising what I thought was a perfect fit to what I had written, I realized that the title could describe topics ranging from HMO billing procedures to a review of the American funeral industry. The cryptic title could also be a comprehensive examination of multi-generational American family units, a look at the federal tax structure, an environmental analysis of graveyards, a review of the worldwide SARS epidemic, or even a biography of the late Senator Strom Thurmond. But the book is none of these things. Strom Thurmond, for example, will (probably) not be mentioned again.

At this point, either your curiosity will get the best of you and you decide to read a few more pages, or you will put the book back on the shelf or in the computer and look for something else because you aren't sure where I am going with this and why take the chance.

If you decide you don't want the book, and you are in one of the nation's surviving bookstores rather than flipping through your Kindle, you would do everyone a favor if you put the book on the nearest table. Every bookstore employee has stories about customers who put the books on shelves where they did not belong. In bookstores, as it is with surgery on the human body, putting something where it does not belong generates problems.

If the act only involved books, I wouldn't mention this pervasive carelessness. But the behavior involves more than books; Americans are careless with articles of clothing, jars of olives, music cd's, small appliances, pretty much whatever they handle. Whether they listen to, wear, or taste the items, Americans lack the ability, or the inclination, to put items back where they belong.

It's not as though we never received training about the desirability of putting things back. Who doesn't remember a constant parental admonition; "Now you put that back where you got it!" But we usually didn't then, and we usually don't now!

In retail stores, fore example, after we decide that we are not buying something, the item turns into a personal irritant that must be discarded as quickly as possible. American consumers would laugh at the idea that they had an obligation to put items back where they got them, never mind what their parents said.

Retail establishments expect this carelessness, and they have learned to live with it. Most organizations include as part of their costs the salaries of employees whose only jobs involve re-shelving errant merchandise. The re-stocking employees prowl the aisles constantly since time may be a vital factor. When a grocery customer decides that the half-gallon of butter pecan ice cream was not a sensible purchase because he is on a low-carb diet and it was an impulse anyway, he might pull it out of his cart and set it on the cookie rack, thinking, if any thought was involved, that cookies and ice cream go together and besides, he is in a hurry. Who knows the logic that inhabits such minds? The stores consider themselves fortunate if that guy doesn't put the ice cream carton on the chicken roasting rack.

By the time he leaves the store, a single consumer could have laid waste to several aisles and dozens of items, and the havoc does not stop there. After using the store's cart to haul the purchases to his car, the customer has to decide what to do with the borrowed shopping cart. He has to push it somewhere so that he can get his car out of the parking space. But though the store supplied the cart for his convenience, it would take too long and be too strenuous to take the cart back to the store.

Many retailers provide what they like to call a *cart return corral* in their parking lots, obviously appealing to the Wild West element in the American psyche. Since the *corrals* usually have very few horses, the psychology does not seem to be working. Drive around any American retail shopping area and you can see abandoned shopping carts scattered over the parking lots like leaves on an autumn day. On windy days, it can be entertaining, if you have a slanted sense of humor, to watch the discarded carts rolling over the asphalt, gathering speed, and headed, for some supernatural reason, toward the newer cars parked in the lot. You can also, if you want to take the time to explore, find grocery carts in vacant lots and apartment building lobbies throughout the surrounding neighborhood.

Some stores designate an employee, either the new guy or someone who has called in sick too many times, as the "shopping cart supervisor." The unfortunate employees wear a vest similar to the type worn by traffic control officers and highway construction workers, although the retail employees lack similar authority. They spend their working hours walking around the parking lot, sometimes even going down the street to the apartment buildings, bringing the store's carts back to the lobby area where they can be picked up and abandoned again. This is a significant problem since the shopping cards cost a lot of money; the nice ones are about one thousand dollars each.

But we were talking about book browsers who do not put books back where they belong. There is probably not a librarian standing, or more likely sitting, who will not, at the drop of a library card, launch into a story about how an important book, maybe one needed by a political science scholar, was improperly re-shelved and lost for years. The librarians will explain that if re-shelving was left completely to patrons, there would be bibliographic chaos; the writings of Descartes might stand next to the recipes of Julia Childs, and Patrick Buchanan's diatribes might be alongside the latest Harry Potter children's novel. Incorrectly shelved books, as any anguished librarian will not hesitate to tell you, are lost books. This is why the signs around libraries and bookstores across the nation urge customers to "just leave the books on the nearest table and we will take care of putting them back on the shelves!"

I do not want to get too far off the subject, although it is already too late for that. But let me try to get back on part of the track. Whatever the title may have implied, the subject of this book is contemporary American society. The various chapters, *essays* might be a better descriptive term, discuss social institutions, issues, and problems that are part of today's world. There are no sinister villains, no diabolical spirits hovering, and no plots involving mysterious people who attend secret meetings in deserted warehouses. The discussions occasionally go off onto what critical readers might define as tangents, but in a book such as this, I mean we are talking about the whole spectrum of human social behavior here, it would be hard to categorize any discussion as a tangent.

The discussions have a slight sociological focus because a sociologist, (me!) wrote them. What is a *sociological focus?* Even after years of teaching the material, I'm not sure how to answer that question. Sociology is, among other things, a rather comprehensive discipline.

One thing that does stand out about sociologists is that we always seem to be mad about something. Sociologists, as individuals who have taken one ore more of the university courses can attest, do a lot of ranting. When they advertise sociology positions, universities should include the stipulation that candidates "must be able to rant and rave." So there will be some ranting in these pages; but I'd like to think it is constructive ranting. Besides, as I have matured, my ranting is far less pronounced than it once was.

And in contrast to other sociological writings, there will be no charts and tables here. I love charts and tables as much as any social scientist, but I also know that if I want anyone other than my friends to read this book, and I'm not even sure about them, I have to find substitutes. In the unlikely event that I need actual data to support an argument, I can put the information in the book's appendix.

The appendix is another fascinating component of a book. I'm not sure why an author puts important material in an appendix. A book's appendix is even more ignored than its introduction. But there is a reason for an introduction. Readers will skim an introductory section because, as I mentioned earlier, they are looking for some insight into the content. And readers who started this section might wonder when and if this insight will come.

But who looks in the appendix? Ever! No one ever goes there. It is every book's private room, the hidden panel, the jeweled ring with a secret code compartment. If the author has a weak or illogical argument, she can get out of the situation or make it seem less tenuous by referring to tables or references that "are in the appendix." You might as well tell your readers that they should take the evening plane to Damascus, find an apothecary by the name of Feisal and ask him for the chart; readers would be as likely to head for Damascus as for the book's appendix, and every author knows this. If a spy wanted a foolproof system for getting documents out of a country, he could use book appendices. Even experienced CIA analysts don't look at book appendices. They know from experience there is nothing there.

What it means then is that readers should not recoil at the prospect of this slight sociological focus to the book. There will be no lines, no arrows, no columns of figures to contemplate, and there will not be anything of significance in the appendix. This book is simply an overview of a few of the major concerns in contemporary American society; or what I see as the major concerns.

I could also describe it as reasonably objective, certainly more objective than Fox Network broadcasts. But like most people, I regard some things as good and other things as not so good. I consider eight-lane highways for example, along with leaded gasoline, global warming, fast food, and religious intolerance as generally bad things. On the other side, I am a big fan of wildlife, clean air, clean water, community theater groups, and of course, books.

I am (relatively) open-minded; I can appreciate a fairly wide range of individual and intellectual perspectives and as a result, I think the discussions here have a good balance. This balance does not mean that every perspective receives equal space; I never thought that ignorance or stupidity merited equal space.

I did not have any personal or political agenda with this book. I did not start out to write a liberal book or a conservative one; but I suppose that readers who consider themselves conservative will be more irritated at the book's content than self-styled liberals might be. Though some of my friends might dispute this, I don't have many *ideological convictions*. I'm not sure I even have any, although that sounds negative. It shouldn't, but people seem to regard personal convictions as important.

Finally, I have no professional connections other than as a sociologist. I do not sit on any corporate boards, I belong to no formal religious groups, and I do not maintain any political party memberships; it might be of passing interest to mention that with the exception of the last two elections, I have rarely voted for a winning candidate. My wife once said that my vote was a guarantee of political defeat. If true, I should have voted for George W.Bush, although it probably would have made no difference since popular votes were not the deciding factor in his first election.

I don't belong to any groups who have regular meetings. I am a card-carrying member of the ACLU, The Sierra Club, Public Citizen, and until recently, the American Sociological Association. The latter does have annual meetings, but I did not attend.

If I had to summarize this book, I would list it as a collection of professional and personal insights, or as much insight as someone with no governmental experience or connections can be said to have. The writing style is balanced, somewhat humorous I think, and with an occasionally caustic tone.

I hope the book will inform, stimulate, and on occasion even irritate readers. In the final analysis, whenever that may occur, I hope that there is something of value here, and that readers regard the experience what many of us would describe as *a good read*.

If not, well, I had good intentions.

CHAPTER 2

Are We Really What We Eat?

● ● ●

OVER THE LAST FEW GENERATIONS, the experts who make good livings explaining social behavior have described the United States as everything from a noble experiment to an oppressive economic machine that grinds people and their dreams into a fine dust. Even if you object to the general assessments, such statements are appealing. We may not like to admit it, but Americans thrive on generalizations; and the more sweeping the generalizations, the more we like it.

We nod our agreement when someone says that "all New Yorkers are rude," or if a friend insists that California residents are "all fruitcakes;" and we laugh (if we are of the male persuasion) when the fellow at the water cooler sums up his home problems by saying, "you know how women are!" And who hasn't nodded when hearing some negative comments applied to all liberals, conservatives, Catholics, Muslims, or Jews?

The appeal is no mystery; people like the strength in broad, unequivocal statements. Narrow statements, filled with wussy qualifications, lack that appeal. American politicians will attest, as much at they ever attest to anything, that voters support candidates who speak with authority. In politics, as in real life, no one wants leaders who sprinkle their pronouncements with terms like *however, sometimes, on some occasions, not always,* and of course, *notwithstanding*. Mitt Romney and his recent presidential campaign would be a good textbook case illustrating the perils of inconsistency. No successful American political candidate is going to get away with "flip-flopping."

But despite their appeal, the all encompassing, *there-are-no-exceptions*, generalizations, about people at least, are invariably wrong. (And before careful readers start wondering; no, there are no contradictions in that statement!) The simplistic generalizations are always wrong because they cannot stand up under serious scrutiny. Maybe not even under non-serious scrutiny. Sociologists, psychologists, political scientists, even economists know that complexities are an inescapable element in human interactions. Human beings may not be completely unpredictable, but they are close. They rarely respond in a manner social scientists predict because even the same person might react differently to the same stimuli on a different day, and even at different times on the same day. Predicting individual human behavior then isn't the same as making astrological predictions, although the success ratio is about the same.

Although there are the distinct differences in individual behavior, we can, if we look carefully, find a few group patterns. People living in what we might describe as *mutual cooperation*, although it would have to be a loose definition of the term, develop similar or at least somewhat complementary sets of attitudes and behavior. The strands of cooperation are essential because no social group, with the possible exception of New Yorkers, could function with everyone doing their own thing. There has to be some awareness for the sensibilities of other individuals in any cohesive group setting.

Even the mythical *Barter Town* had a social structure, with rules and procedures that local residents followed. The rule breakers in Barter Town went into the arena where "two men enter; one man leaves." A crude but apparently effective means of social control. I wondered while watching the movie where they sent two women who had a serious disagreement. But I suppose it doesn't really matter.

If you look closely at Barter Town, or more likely, at places like Chicago or Cincinnati, New York or New Brunswick, and even Los Angeles, you find patterns of acceptable behavior. This commonality exists with attitudes as well, although individual attitudes have more variations. After all, people can think anything they want. In contrast to behavior, attitudes are a *problem* only when the individual elects to translate his attitudes into unsocial behavior. On the occasions when the behavior is unacceptable, the situation may become the responsibility of law enforcement officials. We will talk more about this notion of socially unacceptable behavior later. At least I hope we will.

It is reasonable then to describe community life as a mixing bowl that, with enough stirring, produces a working consistency. The rough spots, lumps if you will, within individuals and groups get pushed down or baked out by daily contact with other people or other groups who are bigger, stronger, more influential or just more obnoxious in pushing their own perspectives. Some rough spots are more persistent than others, so there may be a few bumps left in that societal mix no matter how much stirring we do. In a diverse country like the United States, those bumps can resemble a mountain range. This should about exhaust the cooking metaphors.

If you drive around the United States, (and no one should attempt this without supervision.), you would notice the social bumps. You couldn't miss them. Americans come in a variety of shapes, sizes, and hues, and with major and unresolved differences in attitudes and behavior patterns. The country has groups of Palestinians and Israelis, Croats and Serbs, Indians and Pakistanis, Amish, Catholics, Protestants, Jews, Muslims, and pagans, every conceivable size and shape with every gender and cross-gender represented, most with their own restaurants. The new and not-so-new Americans come from next door and from continents on the other side of the globe. They came to this country, and with some exceptions, they stayed. This persistent attraction of America is worth mentioning, because no matter how deep the nation's problems or how severe the criticism from other points on the globe, people from the other parts of the world still want to come here.

The immigration numbers show the strength of that desire. The United States added fourteen million residents during the decade from 2000-2010, and that growth came from immigration or from the first-generation descendants of earlier immigrants. Virtually every country in the world has representatives living in and around this nation, in Bronx apartments, Chicago bungalows, or Los Angeles split-levels. The new-comers work in every occupation, from dentistry to oil drilling, and from farming to fast food, and they vote for political candidates whose philosophies range from Socialist to Libertarian.

Some immigrants do very well because of their hard work, or good luck, or both, while others labor their whole lives on the economic fringes, hoping that their children will get the break and the fortunes that eluded the parents. All these people, and of course their children, are Americans. Although they cling to a few of their ethnic traditions, in food for example, the immigrants talk, act, speak, and eat, *American*, whatever that may mean. And what that may mean is where we are trying to go; making a few reasonable generalizations about Americans.

What can we say about Americans, a diverse people who are first or second or tenth generation? Is it possible to generalize about such a collection? As one example, the people are all Americans, but does it make sense to insist, as some politicians and preachers enjoy doing, that America is *a family-oriented society*? Before placing Americans into that appealing, "Mom, are there any more cookies?" category, it is important to decide what the term means. Does *family-oriented* mean that Americans put the family social unit first, before friends, jobs, and even before their favorite sports teams?

The data say no. It is difficult, for example, to call the U.S. a family-*oriented* society when approximately 50% of American marriages end in divorce, when twenty-five percent of all children will live in a single-parent household sometime during their lives, and when more than two-thirds of all households with children have both parents working. Children are a major part of any family unit, arguably the major part, so who is watching the kids when both parents work? How family-centered are we when child care is not the highest national priority?

It is also appropriate to consider the high proportion of American children, just about half, being brought up in poverty-level households. How many of the poorer kids are going without life's essentials? What kind of future would anyone predict for children growing up with gaping holes in their educational, social, and perhaps psychological training? We ought to think of such things along with the high levels of domestic and institutional child abuse before joining the persistent chorus of individuals who preach about our family-oriented society.

It is more reasonable to argue that while Americans might endorse the idea that the family is important, there would be considerable variation in how important the family is when it is placed alongside competing claims on the individual's time and loyalty. For example, is the family more important than a long-sought job promotion? Is the family dinner a higher priority than dining out with clients or friends? Is it more important to have a few drinks at a sports bar after work, or to get home in time for an elementary school open house? And would all Americans, the construction workers in New York, the ranchers in Texas, the coal miners in Pennsylvania, the pig farmers in North Carolina, the stock brokers in Chicago, the farmers in Montana, and the skiers in Colorado, answer the questions the same way?

Obviously not. Still, the variations do not mean that the American family is not an important value, if you can follow that tortured phrasing. It would be more accurate, if accuracy rather than hyperbola was the intention, to say that Americans are a diverse group of people with markedly different perspectives on the importance and priority they put on their family life. And you can see now, if you didn't before, how qualified phrasing can cut the heart out of what was once a vigorous pronouncement.

Let's try another direction: Americans might not be as family-oriented as we assumed, but can we say that Americans are the *most generous people on earth?* We can say it, but saying doesn't make it so. When the statement is made, and it often is, it is easy to understand why Americans are quick to agree. It is always nice to hear something good about the country. Who does not like being described as the cutest kid in the first grade class, the best three-point shooter on the high school basketball team, or the sharpest legal mind in firm's corporate merger section? But are Americans that generous? In fact, are they generous at all?

Some of you are already expecting to read that it depends on how we define the word *generous*. And you would be right! One popular definition for generous is based on the presence of a personal conviction that helping other people is important. If you wanted to help other people, and you did a lot of it during the course of your life, the minister or whoever else was summarizing your life, would probably use the term "generous person" in the eulogy. Presumably that would be some comfort to your survivors, if not you.

But in a 1998 attitude survey, less than 10% of a national sample of Americans said that the idea of "helping others "was the *most important* value in their lives. So generosity, or at least the actual act of helping others, is apparently not at the top of America's priority list. If we want to describe Americans as generous, we need a different definition.

According to a 2014 report, Americans donated more than 358 billion dollars. About a third of that was to religious organizations. So approximately 70% of American households made charitable contributions. This proportion sounds impressive, and it may even be generous. After all, when seven out of ten Americans donate money to charity, is this not generous? Maybe, but let's wait until we introduce the notion of motivation. Why individuals give is certainly as important as what or how much they give, at least if the term has any meaning.

If we examine motivation, the generosity picture in the country changes a little. Maybe more than a little. Charitable contributions are also tax deductions. Would the proportion of Americans giving money to charity stay as high if the tax benefits did not exist? The consistent opposition of organized charities to any tax-reform that eliminated charitable deductions argues it would not.

A current radio commercial urges Americans to donate rather than trade-in their older cars, and the announcer lists several useful reasons for making such a gift; first on his list was "avoiding the hassle of selling your car." Then came "the tax advantages." Helping others was last on the list of reasons. This does not seem like the true spirit of generosity.

Statistics show that Americans donate about two percent of their annual incomes to charitable organizations. This proportion does not fit the "give until it hurts" category and it is far from the biblical description of tithing. Although the wealthiest individuals throw more dollars into the charity pot, the rich do not get richer by giving their money away; in fact, they donate less than one-half of one percent of their annual incomes. The Christian Bible says that it is easier for a camel to pass through the eye of a needle than for a rich man to enter the kingdom of heaven. Maybe the wealthier Americans are enjoying themselves while they can.

If giving is a key to heaven, poor people are not going to find it much easier to get through the door. The poorer income groups contribute a higher percentage of their annual incomes to charity, but not that much higher. It is also interesting to note that the *major reason* all people gave for charitable gifts was not because they felt it was appropriate or even necessary, but because "they were asked by someone they knew." The popular reasons for all this giving then detract from what I would define as the spirit of generosity.

How about the periodic global emergencies, when there is a need for food and medical supplies? During such situations, the United States always seems to be the first nation to offer assistance. And the public's response to the terrorist attacks of September 11, 2001 is another indication that there is considerable compassion within the American psyche, is it not?

The easy answer is yes. But it might not be the most complete answer. Although there was a flood of donations to *nine-eleven organizations* after the terrorist attacks, contributions to the other, more traditional charities, dropped dramatically during the same period. Americans were giving a lot to Peter, but at least partly because they gave less to Paul. Many charities were financially hurting because of the declines in their donation receipts after September 11th.

A recent book on the aftermath of the 9-11 attacks also documented the theft and looting that were part of the American reaction. There were also individuals who attempted to profit from the attacks by falsely claiming kinships to people who died. And we should mention the family members who initially refused to accept the financial settlements distributed to the victim families because the money was "not enough."

Of course there was compassion demonstrated in the country after the terrorist attacks. But there were reactions in both directions, ranging from an upward spike in blood donations to violent attacks on mosques and even attacks on American Muslim children going to school. The variety suggests the need for caution before concluding that the nine-eleven episode and its aftermath shows that the United States is the most caring society in the world. It would not be fair to type the country as cruel or heartless, but the country is probably not as kind or generous as we like to think.

Well, if the country is not the most family-oriented or the most generous society in the world, are we the most of anything? Many ministers like to say that Americans are the most religious people in the world. That is, after all, the reason God smiles down on Americans. Or does She?

Answering that question depends, as it always seems to do, on how we choose to define yet another and arguably even more slippery term, *religious*. Although close to twenty percent of Americans say they go to church every week, there is no concrete information on whether or not the people actually went to church. It is possible that they were merely reporting what they usually do, or what they wanted to do but something came up to prevent going to church that particular day; they might have had household chores that could not wait, it could have been the first warm day of the golf season and their first chance to play eighteen holes after a long, cold winter. Or maybe they were out late on Saturday and how many chances do they have to sleep late?

What about the devoted souls who did make the trip to their local houses of worship? Before we sing their praises, it would be appropriate to know how focused they were while they sat in church. Did they pay close attention to the rituals and the sermon, or did their minds wander to other things? It is probably fortunate that rabbis, priests, and ministers do not administer exams to determine what information the attendees actually got from the church services. If ministers gave exams after the church services, something like spot quizzes in a college class, *grading on the curve* could easily become as central to religious salvation as it is to college grade point averages.

There are data (I could say that a chart would be available in the appendix but it isn't!) showing that approximately one-third of Americans either does not go to church, or attends once a year or less. About twenty percent never attend, and about twenty percent go to church regularly.

There are, of course, televised religious programs for shut-ins or those who cannot attend formal services, and the couch-based experiences should probably count for something. Overall though, this pattern of American church attendance does not support the description of an intensely religious society. If we wanted to place the American personality on a religious continuum, we would probably put it somewhere in the middle, somewhere between Mother Theresa and Madonna.

At this point, it seems fair to conclude that there are no easy generalizations about Americans, not if accuracy is important. But what about the country itself? The people and the country, the two apparently similar items are not necessarily the same. The United States, like any large collection of people, has a *collective identity*. The sweeping generalizations about *everyone* in a group (e.g. all married people, all college graduates, all Chicago Bear fans, etc.) are, as we have seen, dubious. But the notion of a collective or social identity is different, and generalizations here will be easier.

All societies are a collection of individuals. But there is more to that mixture than personal characteristics. You can add, subtract, and multiply, apply all varieties of statistical procedures to whatever information you may have about the three hundred and some million individual Americans, and you will still be left without a handle on what *American society* is or is not. It might be helpful to think about that mathematics axiom; the whole cannot be greater than the sum of its parts; but with the society seen as a whole, that sum can be different.

It is this wholeness that makes up the collective identity. Even smaller organizations and groups have group identities. When people call a credit card company with a billing problem, they know that it will not be an easy phone call. Whether they want to remove a disputed charge from their bill or ask (beg!) for extended payment arrangements, they expect problems. Just as there are *difficult people* in the world, there are difficult organizations.

And overall, it is fair to rank credit card companies along with banks as among the more difficult organizations all of us must deal with.

In one of the communities where I lived, it was a pleasure to contact the local library. The people there were anxious to help, whether you called with a question or a problem. I remember one lady working for hours to help with a particularly difficult research question. But that same municipality had a building department that could have come from the bowels of hell. I sometimes wondered if the local government sought out especially insensitive people to staff that particular department. Difficult people may have gravitated to that building department, but it is more likely that the new employees assumed their unpleasant characteristics after they began working there.

When people are at home, they are just people. They are parents, neighbors, friends, teammates in the local bowling league, and consumers. But when they go to work, they cease their roles as loving parents or friendly neighbors and they turn into working parts of an organizational machine. Their individual personalities melt into a collective that overwhelms whatever individual inclinations they have outside that working environment.

Even people with strong personalities blend into their organizational atmospheres because there is no alternative. The pressure is so overwhelming that some workers create a *substitute personality* to use during their working hours. The home personality gets put on a neural shelf and the work or substitute personality takes over during the workday. Individuals do things at work they would never think about doing at home. They say things to customers while sitting at their desks that they would never say to anyone while they sat on their front porches, if they have front porches, or at their dinner tables, if they have dinner tables.

Organizations have collective personalities that exceed, and it might be more accurate to say they *transcend* the people who work there. Production employees, sales people, and even CEO's arrive and depart, buildings will be constructed, painted, or abandoned, product lines emerge and fade, but the company and its identity remain.

The phone company, at least in its earlier monolithic form, was an organization with a strong corporate identity. When people went to work for the telephone company, no matter what their background or gender, they became a *phone man.* They acted like the phone man, and they talked like the phone man. People came to expect certain things from "phone people;" local service organizations often saved a spot in their administration for "the phone company person."

Well-known corporations in contemporary America, Microsoft, Ford Motor Company, AOL/Time Warner, and lest we forget, the late Enron, also have corporate identities. Some corporate personalities are stronger than others, but every organization has one. And employees who go to work for such organizations discover, if they didn't know it before, that their personal identities are overshadowed by the corporate identities.

Kindergarten teachers insist that they can tell what kind of person an individual is going to be, how successful, how creative, or how sociable, all based on what the individual does during the first year of school. If a kindergarten child stands in line without talking, he will adapt to adult social situations. If she colors within the lines, she is destined to be a competent employee, and the kid who regularly sells the most candy in the school's annual fund-raising is going to be a successful corporate executive; as the Arthur Andersen people might have once phrased it; *you can take that one to the bank!*

If you think about it, and you should, it would be nice if societies and business organizations had an educational experience along the lines of the kindergarten experience. If it was possible to train organizations in the same way we socialize children, if we could devise the means to instruct organizations about the rules of reasonable behavior, the entities would learn the same things as the children, the same standards of politeness, the mechanics of how to stand in line, and the rules, such as sharing when playing with others. Violations would have consequences. The offender might have to stand in the corner, or perhaps sit at the *quiet table!* Or the organizational equivalent of the quiet table.

Does anyone else ask themselves, what is so bad about sitting at a quiet table? Although the prospect conjures up negative thoughts in the kindergarten mind, I can't think of a downside to the placement. If my supervisor got mad at something I was doing, or not doing, and said; "I told you not to play any more games of Free Cell on that computer during working hours! Go to the coffee shop and sit in a corner table by yourself! Don't go near a computer even to check your email. You can read, but you cannot talk to anyone!"

This quiet table concept sounds to me like a long coffee break. You play real hard for an hour or so, cut a few sheets of paper, and then start raising a little hell because some other kid took a toy you wanted to play with. So the teacher moves you to the quiet table and you can sit there unmolested for twenty or thirty minutes while you plot your next move. Much like hockey's penalty box, it could be a place to catch your breath before getting back into the game.

I don't want to get any more off the subject than I already am. We were contemplating the notion of business organizations receiving behavior training. Unfortunately, it is not possible to send an entire organization for training. But it would be possible to send the organization's leaders. It is fascinating to contemplate politicians like Mitch McConnell or Ted Cruz being told to sit at the quiet table because they couldn't play nice. Or to imagine Bill Gates being sent to the principal because he wouldn't share. Or the teacher sending Iran's president to the office for playing with scissors. Maybe that quiet table would have made a big difference in the nature of these people, and as a result, in the fates of the organizations they administer.

But all my musings are fantasies, because neither organizations nor societies nor, sadly, the leaders of the organizations, receive training for what they do, or for what they should not do. Random events play the major roles in the development of collective personalities, and an unfortunately common result is the emergence of dysfunctional organizational personalities.

As it is with organizations, so it is with societies. I raised some basic questions earlier about the nature of American society; who, or what, are we? We concluded, or at least I did, that Americans are neither as religious nor as generous as assumed, and there are doubts about how family-oriented we are. A study came out a few years ago listing the ten best nations in the world to have and raise children. The details could be in the appendix, but of course, they are not. Still, it is interesting to mention that the U.S. did not make the best ten list. On the other hand, at least the country was not in the worst ten category either!

At this point, we seem to know more about what we are not than what we are, but this is not a bad thing. Even knowing what we are not helps us better understand what we are, if that bit of analysis helps. But we could get another perspective on the collective American identity from the reactions of people who come to the United States for a visit. As most of us know from personal experiences, visitors can be a useful information source. Visitors form attitudes based on actual experiences; did they enjoy themselves? Was the food good? Were the hosts polite, and were the prices fair? Could they find parking places?

It is an interesting idea, but unfortunately the reactions of U.S. visitors are inconsistent. Tourists describe Americans as very friendly or incredibly hostile, they see us as both helpful and indifferent, and they consider the prices as everything from cheap to outrageous. But we must be doing something right because the visitors continue to come. The United States is one of the primary destinations for the world's tourists; to be completely accurate, the country was recently third, behind France and Spain.

But if we look only at income from tourists, then drawing on the now-immortal words from a recent movie, show *me the money*, tourist money is coming to the United States in bushels. Tourists spend more in the U.S. than in any other country. So either we have more things to buy here, a distinct possibility, or the items we sell are expensive, and who could argue with that? Parking fees alone for a day in New York City could feed a family of six in Somalia for three months.

Speaking of travel, does anyone else miss hitchhiking as a travel option? It was a great way to meet people you otherwise would never have known. It is amazing what thoughts you can share with a complete stranger, or have that stranger share with you, when there is no fear that you will have to discuss or explain what was said. What we had with hitchhiking was a totally non-threatening therapy session. How did the country manage to turn something so productive into something so bad and full of fear?

But getting back to the tourist impressions, their attitudes about the United States vary. But one area where they seem to have strong and more consistent opinions concerns the physical characteristics of their hosts. When asked, visitors frequently mention American physical attributes. Europeans tend to describe Americans as fat people who watch a lot of television. On one occasion, when I was teaching in Denmark and happened to be in an auditorium filled with about two hundred American professionals listening to a lecture on the Danish health system, a colleague leaned over and suggested to me that "there were more fat people in that hall than in the whole of Denmark."

All the discussions about Americans and their waistlines raise an interesting question about the relationship between national diet and this collective personality: is there a connection? When people tell a story about a "short, fat guy," they assume that their listeners understand the kind of person they are describing. A short, fat guy presumably has a markedly different personality from a tall, thin person. People who remember the comedy team of Abbot and Costello will remember that Lou Costello, the little fat guy, was also the stupid, careless one. If a short, fat guy like Lou Costello was what he ate, then can we judge a society by what it eats? Is there a societal equivalent of a short, fat guy?

We think of spicy Mexican food and this is pretty much how we see the Mexican people, as kind of spicy. French cuisine is delicate and expensive, presumably like the average Frenchman. Or Frenchwoman. And anyone who has tasted English food has taken a step in understanding the English. The British Empire once ruled much of the world, with lasting political and economic legacies. Fortunately for the world's gourmands, there was no equivalent British food legacy!

I think it might have been the legendary Julia Childs who said that you could get a lot of insight about people by looking in their pantries. If I opened someone's pantry door and saw three boxes of Hamburger Helper, six boxes of macaroni and cheese, two boxes of powdered milk, twelve cans of green beans, all dented, and six bags of chocolate chip cookies, I could make some generalizations about that household. I know I would want to go to a restaurant rather than sit down to a home-cooked meal.

Unfortunately, we don't have a national pantry, although there is Nebraska. But there are a few food items that represent a typical, or at least a frequent American meal, and the nature of those typical foods is interesting. American mealtime is different from many other parts of the world. Europeans, for example, see their mealtimes as special, a period for leisure and reflection. A French dinner or a Danish lunch, they are not just calorie intake sessions; they are major social events in the day.

But not in the United States. We don't linger over our food. We usually want our nourishment fast, because we have other things to do. The taste is almost incidental. Americans spend 110 billion dollars a year on fast food with no sign of a decline, and that expenditure illustrates how unimportant taste is to the American palate. If there still is an American palate.

Dinner at a French restaurant conjures images of a well-dressed couple sitting down to a presentation of quail on toast spears, perhaps with three asparagus stems circling the plate in a kind of green embrace. Wine, of course, would be mandatory. A similar scenario for an American meal would be a couple, both in t-shirts and blue jeans, who order their meals to go and eat while driving to the movie.

America's pantry focuses on fast food, and, not incidentally, a lot of it. The immense quantities underlie at least part of our national weight problem. More than one-third of Americans are seriously overweight. The public reaction to the periodic announcements is to criticize the studies. There is no nice way to say it; many Americans are fat. Far too many of us are walking around carrying enough extra weight to be two of us. .

The situation is worse for the children. It is frightening to examine the obesity figures for kids. No one in school sings the "fatty, fatty, two by four, can't get through the bathroom door" anymore because overweight kids are no longer the exception. The health implications are serious, and the kids are also developing lifestyle patterns that last a lifetime. And their lifetimes are destined to be shorter, less active, and far less enjoyable than they would otherwise have been.

Food is only part of the obesity problem. The other component and another part of this American identity we want to pin down involves lifestyle patterns, or how people occupy their time. We could describe the American lifestyle as *sedentary*, but that would be too vague; lazy might be more accurate! Few Americans get any degree of physical activity or regular exercise. This observation has nothing to do with joining exercise clubs or buying treadmills, nor is it an indictment of the growing service economy. A key part of the problem is that Americans don't even have much physical activity in their daily lives.

Because of their jobs and the labor-saving devices in their homes, Americans don't have to do much physical exertion. And partly as a result, they don't want to do anything strenuous. Who knows which came first? What we do know is that many Americans shun any type of physical effort. They take elevators instead of climbing stairs, they circle the mall parking lot for an hour looking for a space close to one of the entrances, they use a gas blower to rake their leaves, they never walk when they can drive, and they find reasons to rent a cart when they play eighteen holes of golf. Americans seem to put physical exertion on the same desirability plane as dental appointments.

Americans are not playing softball or tennis when they are not at work, so what are they doing during their leisure hours? They apparently spend a lot of their relaxation hours watching television. Almost half of the American households have three or more televisions and approximately two-thirds of Americans spend between two and six hours a day watching a television schedule that is about as nutritious as fast food.

Taking a closer look at the American activity clock, if we take four hours of daily television viewing as the national average, add eight hours a day for work, three hours for commuting, an hour for eating three meals (fast food, remember!), an hour for personal hygiene, and eight hours for sleeping, most American adults wake up each day already owing an hour. No wonder they are always in a hurry.

Looking then at family values, religious behavior, charitable inclinations, individual Americans and America as a country are both difficult to describe or categorize. If we wanted a quick summary for the country's collective identity, we could do worse than use food as a metaphor. Then it might be accurate to describe the collective American personality as a cheeseburger with everything, and French fries.

To go!

CHAPTER 3

Excuse Me?

● ● ●

How MANY TIMES IN OUR daily encounters with other people will they suggest that we "have a nice day?" By some estimates, mine at least, we hear that statement about ten times every day, more if we visit retail establishments. Some of us get to the point where we wouldn't mind having a bad day just to spite people.

There are variations in that phrase, and that diversity keeps the declaration from becoming even more annoying than it already is: "Have a good day," "enjoy your day," and the abbreviated, "have a good one." I suppose that the substitutes serve some purpose for the speakers. What intrigues me is not so much the wording as what people really have in their minds when they make the statements.

Does anyone else wonder why people don't say "good afternoon or "good evening anymore? And we don't hear, "thank you for stopping by," or even the sometimes unsettling, "good luck to you." Why do I need good luck? Does she know something I don't know?

Gone also are, "it was nice talking to you," "take it easy," "see you soon," and my personal favorite, "take it slow!" "Later," has also fallen into disuse, maybe because of the potential for unfavorable images conjured up in the minds of the listeners when they heard that single word. All the presumably obsolete phrases, focused on a means of saying "good by," albeit in different fashion, have moved to wherever it is that discarded phrases go. With all the available pronouncements, why did anyone feel the need for new ones? The new ones arguably are no better and might be considered not as good. Unfortunately, we will probably never know exactly why no one says "later" anymore.

Whatever the reasoning, that new phrase in all its forms is here and apparently to stay, for the time being anyway. And as I mentioned earlier, it is interesting to ponder its' frequent use. Is it reasonable to assume that the individuals who say "have a nice day," really want us to have one? How important is it to them? Will they try to help our pursuit of a better day?

If we accept the interpretation that the speakers want their listeners to have a nice day, then it would say something positive about personal sensitivities as well as the level of social courtesy in this country. This courtesy level, in case the reader was beginning to wonder where I was going with this discussion, is what interests me. What about American courtesy? Are we courteous to one another? Do visitors from far away places with strange sounding names leave with a warm and fuzzy feeling about American courtesy? When they leave, do they think along the lines of, "wow, what a nice bunch of people the Americans are?"

The questions are not easy to answer, especially the fuzzy part. Let's focus for a moment on that "have a nice day!" phrase. If we use the one hundred million adults who daily prowl the nation's shopping arenas as a base number, and each of the shoppers hears the words ten times during their shopping, then the statement is made in America approximately one billion times each day. If people mean what they say, it seems fair to conclude that there is a lot of courtesy out there in the country's hills and valleys. On the other hand (and you knew there was going to be one,), that conclusion might be premature.

Before we examine the question of how much or how little courtesy Americans have, and you might be surprised to see just how slippery that question is, we should define the key term: what is *courtesy*? Webster defines courtesy as "a polite or courteous act," but Mr. Webster does not explain what a "courteous act" is.

Does courtesy occur when someone utters a few words to another individual, perhaps an "excuse me!" along with a half smile when he cuts into a theatre line, as though that explained everything? Or does courtesy require more effort? There is a argument that courtesy is not an easy trait to measure because it is not a question of yes or no, it is or it is not, but exists in varying amounts, something like financial security, or patriotism. I hope readers are following this!

There is, for example, what we could describe as a low degree of courtesy. The *LDC* occurs when people allow someone to butt in the grocery checkout line because she is carrying a small child. Or a large child. Or when they allow a fellow motorist to pull his car in front of theirs during a traffic jam. LDC's are more common than acts at the other end of the spectrum because they are fairly easy. When you are having one of your good days, LDC's are as easy as, well as falling off of that log. Although there are not many of us that have ever fallen off a log.

Then there are what we are going to call, because we can call them anything we want, High Degrees of Courtesy (HDC's). If an individual pulled over to the side of the road to help a fellow motorist who had his car hood in the air and steam was coming out of the engine, that would be an example of a HDC. And obviously, there are points on the continuum between the two extremes.

So we have established that there are degrees of courtesy. This will probably be the last point of agreement on the topic. We have clarified some, though certainly not all, of Webster's definitional problems. Here is another troubling point; would people define courtesy the same way in Chicago as they might in Chattanooga? Do residents of New York City have the same courtesy standards as, well, anywhere else in the world? Are courtesy standards similar throughout the country or for that matter, throughout the world? Our instincts tell us "no," and the instincts are, at least this time, correct.

Politely standing in line, *queuing up* they call it, is normal and expected from Englishmen and women. When there are crowds of people waiting for tickets, whether for seats on the bus on in a theatre, the English generally stand politely in line and wait their turn. The Danes would laugh at this behavior. In Denmark, the head of the line belongs to the most nimble or to the strongest, and you could starve to death in Copenhagen waiting for someone in the restaurant line to say, "Go ahead! You were here first."

If we had to place the United States along that courtesy continuum, most of us, if we were honest, would put our country closer to Denmark than to England. Although we have no specifics on how many times people show a lack of line courtesy, we can all conjure up some unpleasant experiences. Recently I was sitting in the waiting room of a hospital laboratory. Several people, including me, were sitting around a typically uncomfortable *waiting room*, flipping through the old magazines (does any hospital waiting room anywhere have new magazines?) waiting for the clerk to open the sliding glass window.

We all knew who had arrived first (me!), and the rest of the five or six individuals arriving afterwards knew their place. Survival in an urban setting requires some basic skills, one of which is knowing your turn when you are waiting. The first thing any sensible person does when he enters a waiting situation is determine where he belongs and then prepare to do what he must to claim his rightful spot.

But on occasion, the normal rules of engagement will not apply. When the hospital technician finally opened the glass window, at two minutes past the posted opening time, and yelled out, "who's first?" the stampede was immediate. There was no courtesy, nothing close to it. No one stood to the side letting the other guy go first because everyone wanted out of that room and out of that hospital as quickly as possible. We would have made even the Danes look polite. One elderly lady with a bad hip was pushed to the side as though she had been a traffic cone.

Now we can expand the definition and define courtesy as a *demonstrated deference to the needs or sensibilities of others*. The discerning reader recognizes that this definition, like Mr. Webster's, has its limitations. But it does have more direction than Webster provided. Using this definition, if individuals go out of their way to consider someone else's sensitivities, they are courteous.

This means that the mere use of words will not qualify. The bottom line is that all the millions of "have a nice day!" statements we discussed at the outset mean nothing. (Most readers knew this was going to happen!) No strokes in the courtesy category, no hash marks on sleeves, nothing, because if the term *courtesy* is to have any meaning, it cannot be applied with the reckless abandon that characterizes terms such as charisma, hero, or weapons of mass destruction. In this context at least, we are going to use deeds, not words, to assess courtesy. Watching what people do and not what they say, as the immortal John Mitchell once remarked, is the best way to assess performance.

There are criteria other than action that could be useful in assessing courteous behavior. For one thing, the behavior should be spontaneous. The requirement for spontaneity means that courteous individuals are making impulsive decisions to consider the needs or sensitivities of others. The perpetrator, if I can use that term, would not have his courtesy dictated by rules posted on a door or bulletin board. This means, for example, that employees in a supermarket who are required to help customers with their groceries are not being courteous; they are following the rules.

Next, there should be no enforcement unit for courteous behavior. Even if there are no posted rules about what people should do, individuals are not being courteous, not in the sense in which I am defining it here, if they are penalized, or rewarded, for their actions. A number of retail organizations monitor their incoming customer telephone calls to provide what they describe as *quality control*. What we are calling courtesy then will not include such telephone conversations, high quality or not. We are looking for a spontaneous act whose only reward is the perpetrator's sense of satisfaction.

Truly courteous behavior should also require some effort. If the behavior requires no energy, we might describe the act as nice, but it would not fit our definition of courteous. Smiling at a stranger as you walk down the street is a nice gesture, but it is not courteous. We all know that it takes more effort to frown than to smile.

As long as we are dealing with effort, there is also the issue of legality. Sometimes people make an effort to consider the needs of others but it has nothing to do with courtesy and everything to do with legal behavior.

Letting the oncoming traffic get through the intersection before you make your left-hand turn is not courteous any more than allowing the pedestrians to cross before you complete your right-turn is. The actions merely conform to what the law demands.

Finally, to be counted as courteous, the behavior should require the sacrifice of self-interest. Another way of putting it is that the act should be somewhat inconvenient for the perpetrator. We can return to the grocery store for an example because they are as close to laboratories as social scientists usually get. When the clerk who bags the groceries separates the soap products from the fruits and vegetables, and then puts the bread on top, there is no inconvenience or sacrifice involved from that clerk. The actions simply demonstrate proper training in the art of bagging. On the other hand, if that same clerk finished an order and then ran out into the rain to catch a shopper who forgot a can of oysters, that action represents sacrifice and we could describe the act as courteous.

Now we are moving along with refining this definition. We have three rules for courteous behavior; spontaneity, effort, and sacrifice, three more than we had before we started. There are still a few problems; vagueness and overlapping of the three criteria come to mind, but the three stipulations allow us to screen out actions that we might otherwise include in what would have been a distorted image of American courtesy. We are now in a much better position to ask about the level of social courtesy.

So back to that question; how courteous are Americans? There is no better place, with the possible exception of grocery stores, to begin the analysis than on the nation's roadways. When Americans are in their cars, they are in their private kingdoms. At least, this is how drivers see the situation. There is no other authority behind that wheel. Although the driver cannot perform marriages, in every other respect he sees himself as the captain of the ship. What the driver says, or does, goes. If the driver wants to go faster, he presses the accelerator. He does not have to submit the request to a committee, he does not have to check with his boss, and he does not have to file a report to justify the procedure. Unless he is exceeding the posted speed limit and some law enforcement authority is watching.

But the driver is still the king of his road and master of everything on the horizon. If he wants to move to the other lane, cutting off a slower and more careful driver in the process, he can do it. And he might do it because he can do it!

With all this unrestricted authority and the almost unlimited opportunity for independent movement, how many American drivers show courtesy on the road? What prevails on the nation's highways, good or bad manners?

Most readers are already laughing, and the remainder is probably chuckling. No one who regularly drives on American's roadways views the situation out there as anything but chaotic and mean-spirited. There is more courtesy during a European soccer brawl than on American roadways. I once talked to a woman who drove fifteen miles out of her way every working day so that she could avoid the expressway. "They will never let me merge," was her explanation.

It wasn't that many years ago that if you had car trouble, you pulled over to the side of the road and waited for help. And help usually came, sometimes from a trucker but just as often from a fellow citizen. When I was on my way back to an Army base years ago, I was driving the used car I had just purchased. I was in the middle of the Kentucky hills when smoke started pouring from under the hood and the car came to a stop. The engine was running, but the car wouldn't move.

There I was, at five o'clock on a Sunday evening, it was getting dark, and I was stuck on a Kentucky hillside and due back on the base in North Carolina by nine the next morning. I can still remember how desperate I felt. In just a few minutes, another car pulled to the side of the road and the couple asked if they could help. The couple couldn't fix my car, but they did take me to their friend's service station. And although he was in the process of closing, the owner got in his tow truck and hauled my car to one of his repair bays. It didn't take him long to see that the clutch was burned out. When I told him that I was due back on post by the next morning, he called his friend at the auto parts store, went over and got the new clutch, and then spent several hours installing it.

It was at that point that I realized I had no money to pay for his efforts. This was in the days before universal credit cards. "No problem," the guy said to me. "Just send me the money when you have it."

Would the same thing happen today? Every reader is laughing now. If your car has trouble on the road today, police advise you to roll up your windows and run up a distress flag. If a passing motorist stops to ask you if they could help, you are advised to lock your windows and ask the person to call the police. You are not even supposed to make eye contact with the people who are trying to help.

I was kidding about the eye contact, but there is no kidding involved in describing the nation's roads as places you'd rather not be. Pulling off the road for some sleep, even in a camper designed for such things, is illegal now, as authorities try to limit the number of assaults on parked cars by limiting the number of parked cars. It is hard to quarrel with that logic. Even when burley truckers pull off the road to catch a few hours sleep, they do so only in packs, like the Wildebeests on the Serengeti Plain. And keep in mind, they are the *burley truckers*! It is hard to imagine what scrawny drivers are supposed to do.

You can get in trouble on the nation's highways even without parking. If you happen to offend another motorist by driving too slowly or if you change lanes too quickly and cause another motorist to spill his coffee, you could be the newest victim in what is now described as "road rage." Many people see examples of this rage each time they venture out in their cars. Drivers, angry at being cut off, start chasing the offender. Other drivers, irritated at the slow pace of the car in front, start harassing the slowpoke by tailgating or flashing their highway lights. It is not unusual for items to be thrown from one car at another and on occasion, the drivers get out of their car to confront one another, sometimes with tragic results.

So how much courtesy is there on American roads? About the same level as we might find in a Roman chariot race. Film buffs can conjure up the race scene in *Ben Hur*, to imagine what it is like driving to work during rush hour in any major city. Individuals who are not film buffs will just have to do without the image. Americans average almost twenty million automobile accidents each year. Four million people are injured and more than forty thousand killed each year in the accidents.

When I was thinking about this particular point, I looked at the 1993 statistics from automobile accidents; there was no particular reason for choosing that year, but what the hell, it was as good as any other year. In that year, there were 46,836 accidents, and with a few judgments and occasionally tenuous assumptions, I decided that more than half of such accidents resulted from a lack of courtesy. The causes ranged from improper turns to hit and run, or to describe it in a fashion never seen in traffic court, a lack of reasonable courtesy. That percentages sounds high, but after driving on American roadways for thirty years, I am surprised that the carnage isn't higher.

American drivers, as I mentioned earlier, are people who are anxious to get where they are going. What makes them different from other anxious people is that the drivers are armed with several tons of metal. Americans live fast lives, they drive large, fast cars, and in their harried minds, people who delay them from their assigned tasks deserve no consideration or courtesy. If you had the opportunity to talk to the drivers, and you should not attempt to do this without supervision, they would likely tell you that they didn't have time to be courteous. It seems reasonable to conclude that there is no significant degree of courtesy on America's roadways.

Here is strike one!

But we should look at other locales before drawing any conclusions. Behavior at sporting events is a good potential source because of the opportunity for spontaneity. What could be more spontaneous than behavior at the nation's baseball, football, hockey, and PGA tournaments? People can sit, relax, eat hot dogs, and enjoy themselves. In the process, they expose their emotions. The chance to show emotion at the events is, after all, half the fun. Maybe more than half! So if Americans were courteous at their sporting events, it would be a plus on their social report cards.

Once again, readers are trying to muffle their chuckles. Anyone who has attended major sporting events is likely to be laughing hysterically. Unfortunately for our analysis, there are no available data about spectator behavior at sporting events. We do not know, for example, if contemporary football fans who paint their faces and spend their time screaming obscenities at the officials are qualitatively different from the people who decorated their togas to watch gladiator games in early Rome. Did the Romans even paint their faces? We may never know.

What we do know from fairly widespread impressions is that the behavior of contemporary sports fans is, in general, not kind. It is a long way from courteous behavior. There was an incident years ago involving hundreds of football fans who threw bottles and cans at referees in an NFL game. The Baltimore team owner was unapologetic, explaining that the local fans just "cared about their team." Apparently the fans cared more about the team than they cared about the health of the officials on the field.

Exuberance about their team doubtlessly also explains the two fans who jumped onto a baseball field during a baseball game and attacked the first base coach. The fans later explained that they had too much to drink and they were mad about their team losing. The latter excuse was particularly weak since they were Chicago Cub fans, a group that should have become accustomed to losing. Not incidentally, this dynamic duo wanted to be on television. The one positive element in this ugly incident was that it was a father and son who attacked the coach. At least the assault was a family activity.

Sometimes the discourteous behavior doesn't occur on the playing field. Until the 2002 season, the Chicago Bears played their NFL home games in a rather ancient stadium on the city's lakefront. The stadium was a national landmark, at least until the city decided to modernize it. But that interesting political story has nothing to do with courtesy.

Like many older buildings, Soldier's Field did not have enough toilet facilities. It sometimes makes you wonder if our grandparents had stronger bladders. Anyway, fans at football games drink a lot of beer, and they seem to need the comfort facilities at the same time. According to newspaper reports, it was not unusual for impatient fans to start rocking the porta-potty when the individual inside took too long to perform his functions. It is hard to imagine the pressure on the poor guy in that facility, and it is impossible to categorize the behavior of the people who rocked the boat so to speak as anything but insensitive. It was definitely not courteous. Strike two against American courtesy!

But most Americans do not attend professional sports events. And it would be unreasonable to conclude that only discourteous Americans go to sporting events or that everyone attending a sporting event is discourteous. Before attempting even tenuous conclusions, we should have another location where Americans express their feelings without consulting a posted list of rules. What better place to look than the nation's shopping malls? No officials, no rules, and no penalty calls!

If we watch the activity in shopping malls, it would make us yearn for the relative calm of an NFL playoff game or even the rest rooms at a Chicago Bears game. When people attend sporting events, they want to enjoy themselves. They are fairly relaxed. Shoppers, however, are people in a hurry. They want to get their items and move to the next sale. If something, or someone, delays that movement, shoppers show as much patience as automobile drivers. If you think about it, and you probably should, American mall shoppers are automobile drivers without the cars.

Although mall behavior is always interesting, the Christmas holiday season is unique. Every holiday season produces stories of shoppers fighting over the latest "must-have" toys, or trying to get a sweater in a certain size. My favorite incident from the last few years occurred in a Midwestern supermarket, where several fellow shoppers beat a woman because she brought more than fifteen items into the express lane. "She got what she deserved," many readers might be thinking at this point. But was this situation not appropriate for some courtesy? Perhaps that harried shopper had a sick child at home. Or she could have been doubled-parked. In any case, this is an easy call against American courtesy: Strike three!

Not much courtesy is evident in the retail marketplace, but what about traveling behavior? How, for example, do people behave when they are in an airplane? Veteran travelers know that American air carriers stack their passengers like processed potato chips, with little room for leg or hip movement let alone comfort. The degree of physical discomfort is matched by internal air quality that is something like a sixth grade gym locker. The food, when it is served, is at its best, only moderately digestible.

With all the discomfort, airline travel qualifies as an ideal location for assessing courtesy. After all, people should be at their best when their surroundings are the worst. Who can forget the classic example of traveling courtesy, the Titanic passengers sitting at their dinner tables drinking fine wine while the ship went down? Well done, I would have said had I been there, although I would have doubtlessly yelled the comment as I headed for the lifeboats.

Airline attendants are the best source for information about passenger behavior. Their stories are both fascinating and frightening. Passengers urinating on beverage carts because of a delay in getting a drink, people sneaking into the airplane bathrooms for illicit smokes, or passengers on the brink of rioting because of a delay in the flight's departure, airline attendants can provide a thousand stories to support their contention that passenger courtesy is an illusion. Many airlines routinely provide their cabin attendants with handcuffs to use on unruly passengers, more evidence, if we need it, about the low courtesy levels there. Strike four!

Finally, in this examination of American courtesy, we can look at behavior in arenas such as restaurants and movie theatres, places where people go to relax. When people go to restaurants, they are not shopping, they are not yelling for their local sports team, they generally will not have to wait for the bathroom, and they will not be sitting in an airline seat. All things considered, people should be fairly relaxed and, it seems fair to conclude, more sensitive to the needs and interests of their peers.

Almost anyone who goes to a theater will agree that the courtesy level in the theatres is about the same as you find outside of a sports stadium bathroom. Insensitivity toward others is the rule not the exception. After every movie, you can find food scattered around the floor, the result of candy, sandwiches, and popcorn being dropped or discarded during the movie. And is there anyone out there who hasn't stepped on gum on a theater floor?

And who has not been bothered by movie patrons who bring crying babies or ringing cell phones into the theater? The latter is such a common occurrence that theatres routinely publish announcements on the screen asking patrons to turn their instruments off before the movie begins. We remember that if they have to ask for courteous behavior, by our rules, it doesn't count!

Even the people who don't bring cell phones or small children can exhibit their lack of courtesy by talking during the movies. Some people seem to save their discussions until the best parts of the movie. The same people persistently ask questions of their companions while the movie is still going on: "What did she mean by that?" "What did he say?" or "Doesn't that guy look just like Ernie from high school?" Strike five!

Driving, sports events, shopping, eating out or going to the movies, despite the absence of what some would call *hard data*, there is considerable anecdotal evidence that courtesy in American life is uncommon. Americans seem to agree with this assessment, and they often insist that things were better *in the old days*. It's a comfortable idea that everything, and everyone, "used to be much nicer."

Maybe they did. And maybe Americans were nicer at one time. And it is possible that we could learn to be more sensitive to the needs of our fellow citizens. We might think about this desire for more courtesy as we drive to work, when we are waiting in a bathroom line, when we are about to get on a plane, or when we are sitting in the theatre. We might. And we might not.

Anyway, have a good one!

Later!

CHAPTER 4

People Don't Know How to Behave Anymore!

● ● ●

WE ALL HAVE CHILDHOOD MEMORIES. Well, most of us do. Some of the memories are more pleasant than others, and it is interesting, sometimes, listening to what emerges when people dig around in their memory banks. The human mind is like a psychological landfill, a place where all sorts of unusual and occasionally interesting things have been discarded.

Some of us have only good memories. Childhood conjures up images of cold lemonade, Toll House cookies fresh from the oven, and regular trips to the ballpark with Uncle Fred. The happy childhood people were the hall monitors in elementary school, they ran for student council offices in high school, they majored in economics or psychology in college, and often went into politics or television talk shows where they could instruct other people how to behave so that their lives would be similarly blessed.

The *other, less happy ones* have more varied memories. We remember episodes sometimes less heart-warming than cookies from the oven. It seems fair to say that for most people, childhood was a blend of both the good and the bad. And when we were bad, the punishment may have been nothing more than someone yelling about *behaving properly*. We might have been careless with a piece of living room furniture or teased a younger sibling, or got caught sneaking a puff from one of Uncle Joe's cigars.

Maybe we played with our food during a family dinner, or fooled around with household equipment not designed for children. The vacuum cleaner comes to mind as equipment that always offered intriguing possibilities for inquiring minds. When such things happened, Mom, Dad, the teacher, or even Uncle Joe, would be shaking a finger in your direction and asking whether you knew how to behave. Historians should trace the origin for finger wagging as a form of behavior control for children. Why did anyone ever think it would work? Did it ever work? Did the Romans shake their fingers at their kids? Did the Neanderthals?

But getting back to that notion of behaving, even after years of social science teaching and writing, I am not sure what people mean when they say, *behave yourself.* I doubt that even the speakers know what they mean. I am sure they know the implied meaning, but children are not especially good at ferreting out nuances in vocabulary. Not that the adults are any better.

Let's expand on that ambiguous admonition about behaving. Because whether the child is eating her dinner or throwing it against the wall, even if she is using that fascinating household vacuum cleaner to suck the tropical fish out of the tank, she is behaving. This is what Mom and Dad said they wanted.

Even if the child set fire to the family garage, threw a chair through the living room picture window, or flushed the family's vacation tickets down the toilet, all the episodes constitute behaving. Outside observers might define the actions as destructive or harmful, but, and I don't want to belabor the point, although I may already have, the kids are behaving!

Whatever the adult may have said, what that person really wants is for the child to behave *in an acceptable fashion.* People expect children, and for that matter they expect other adults, to behave as positive and contributing parts of an organized and civil society. Although this explanation provides some clarification about what *behave yourself* means, it does not answer questions about the guidelines people contemplate when they visualize *acceptable behavior.* Who established the guidelines? What were the criteria for adopting them? And what exactly are the rules we are supposed to follow when we are behaving ourselves in this more acceptable fashion?

A logical place to begin answering such questions would be finding the source. I don't mean the source for specific rules such as not blowing your nose into a restaurant dinner napkin, at least not while other people are eating, but the origin of the perceived need for rules. Why do people need rules anyway? We have to go way back for the answer, before there were trained historians to record what people were doing. Or not doing.

Somewhere about the time that humans started sharing their living areas with other members of the species, they developed a set of expectations about how the other people in the group needed to behave. Humans decided early in their co-habiting process that certain types of behavior were functional and other types were not. For example, a person in a leadership capacity probably concluded early on, and I know it would have been one of the first things I would have been thinking about, was that it was not good when other residents threw bones, other food scraps, and who can guess what else into the community sleeping areas.

Another leader, and I am guessing that his or her suggestion was also one of the first to be adopted, concluded that it was in everyone's interests if individuals went outside the living area to take care of their personal toileting. The expectations about what passed for personal hygiene back then were probably among the earliest rules for acceptable behavior.

Although many of the earlier rules have either disappeared or have become so thoroughly ingrained in our lives that we no longer think of them as *rules*, the fundamental principle underlying their emergence and persistence is the same; when humans live together, they have expectations about how other people in the community are supposed to behave. The expectations emerge because there is no alternative to social cooperation. Without some rules governing interactions such as business transactions and personal disputes, no group would advance beyond the most primitive existence. Without cooperation, our species would still be hunting and gathering and fighting over every scrap of food, every sharp rock, and every comfortable cave. We might not admit it, and a few people don't seem to like the idea, but humans rely on one another's cooperation. We have to have it!

It is this cooperation that leads to the formation of what we can describe as the rules of social engagement. With rules and standards for behavior, members of a society know what is expected. And they know what to expect of others. Some type of framework for acceptable behavior in societies emerged then not because there was any sermon, a formal committee meeting, or a congressional investigation. Cooperation came because cooperation works better than constant disputes.

The rules are frustrating at times, but the rules make life easier for everyone. And because they make people's lives easier, people come to accept and even internalize the rules. "Of course you can't take something that doesn't belong to you! Everyone knows that!" With time, and the arrival of still more group members, there are even more rules and the range of acceptable behavior changes. Some times, the range gets larger. More often, it gets smaller.

Some behavior patterns disappear because they are no longer relevant or useful. A loud belch at the end of a meal once indicated a guest's pleasure, a sign both of a full stomach and general contentment with the food. If a guest did not belch, it was an insult to the host. Even a belch from the lower portion of the digestive tract was acceptable, a tradition that Benjamin Franklin extolled in his published work, *Fart Proudly*. Franklin's admonition mercifully has died out, and currently no one can fart proudly, even in fast food restaurants.

Some behavior patterns persist even though their meaning has changed. During the plague years of the Middle Ages, a sneeze was a sign that the individual was expelling harmful elements. If you sneezed, your companions would be likely to mutter, "God blessed you." Obviously a sneeze today has nothing to do with the plague, not usually anyway, and although a sneeze will still prompt more than a few "God bless you's," from a crowded room, it is unlikely that the well wishers were thinking about the plague.

So some of our behavior has its roots in history. We do something because we have always done it and our parents did it too, if that makes sense. This skips the important question of "why," but there are not always conclusive answers to that question. Not here anyway.

There are other factors contributing to our behavior standards. Our genetic pool, for example, plays a part in our behavior, but it is difficult to assign a precise proportion to this component. 'You're acting just like your father," is an admonition that can ignite flares in young minds.

Do we have any idea what proportion of human behavior our genes determine? The answer depends on who you ask. Sociologists sometimes claim that if society gave them one hundred babies, and everyone should be thankful that this remains a remote possibility, they could raise one hundred lawyers, one hundred accountants, or one hundred politicians. I'm not sure which of the outcomes is the scariest, but the claim implies that it is environmental rather than genetic influences that have the dominant role in human behavior. That argument between nature and nurture, familiar to anyone who has taken a social science course, has never been settled. With the emerging data we now have about how genes can be modified by the environment and the altered genes transmitted to the next generation, it is reasonable to say that human behavior is part genetic and part environmental. And the disputes continue.

There is general agreement though that one important influence on behavior is the family. There are the family genes of course, but we are talking now about social values and learned behavior. The family unit is the earliest influence on the infant. The family is often the only influence during this initial and critical period. The individual's family sets a pattern that, for some individuals, is never broken.

The family can continue this learning dominance during the child's growing years. Factors such as friends and fellow workers emerge at different times during the individual's life, but the family remains influential. The old adage that *an apple never falls far from the tree,* is grounded, if I can use that term, in the family's importance to what happens to a person.

Formal education is another key player in the behavior equation. *Everything I need to know I learned in Kindergarten,* a popular book from years ago, argued that most of the individual's real education was concentrated in the early school years. By the time they get to college, most people already know everything. Or they think they do. Either way, people's minds are often hardened by the time they leave high school and that is a scary thought.

In addition to family and school influences, work, neighborhoods, volunteer organizations and friendships all have a part in shaping individual behavior. This varied input, and it might be reasonable to compare it to cooking, can produce some very different products. The same recipe in different hands turns out distinctly different results.

The input can also produce some confusion for the person who is trying to behave. Who are you supposed to listen to when people around you are telling you to behave yourself, but have very different ideas of what you are supposed to be doing? The teacher, Mom, Uncle Joe, the church minister, your best friend from down the street, the people may be telling you different things about what you should be doing. When you think about it, with all the voices clamoring for recognition, it is amazing that anyone does anything right. Or that they would know it if they did.

The individual can behave in a fashion that is fine at home, but he will be criticized for doing it at school. She can tell a story that will produce chuckling around the office water cooler, but receive clucks of disapproval in her sister's living room. When a friend of mine was in college, he regularly entertained his fraternity brothers by placing a match next to his rear end and expelling gas that would have made Benjamin Franklin, if not the Sierra Club, proud. The resulting flaming spectacle was so entertaining that the fraternity kept a supply of canned pork & beans on hand so that the fire show would be available on demand.

Although this demonstration was much admired by the fraternity house residents, it is hard to imagine another acceptable locale. Church groups, a Kiwanis meeting, the local Chamber of Commerce, the Young Republicans, is it possible to even conceive of another place where this guy could have brought out his match book and found an appreciative audience?

That illustration is probably not typical, but it makes the point that our society contains a variety of people and organizations telling us what we can and should do, and the inputs are rarely consistent. It is amazing how most of us manage to get through our lives without too many conflicts.

Speaking of the potential conflicts, there is an organization that excels at minimizing behavioral conflicts, an organization that has no confusion about how or what it defines appropriate behavior. I refer to the U.S. Army. The example will not surprise anyone who has spent time in that organization. The army is a perfect illustration of what, in social science circles anyway, is described as a *total institution.*

The military bureaucracy, employing approximately one million people and with no product to speak of other than war maintains an amazing level of efficiency. The army removes thousands of civilians from the nation's streets every year without any intense screening. A high school diploma, or the equivalent, and a pulse are usually enough to get you into the American army. In good economic times, when it is more difficult to lure individuals into the rigors of military service, the army relaxes even those standards. The resultant variety in the talents of the incoming recruit groups would be enough to give nightmares to corporate trainers.

The army's new employees appear for their first day dressed in everything from motorcycle jackets to suit jackets, more of the former than the latter, wearing rings on every possible appendage, and brimming with young adult hormonal levels. Yet in a few short weeks, the army turns the individuals and their hormones into functioning parts of cohesive units.

As any CEO can attest, group cohesiveness is not an easy accomplishment. Some companies have their employees for more than thirty years and despite working alongside one another during that time, the work units do not come close to becoming cohesive. How many times have we heard our friends and relatives complain that though they worked for an organization many years, they "never felt as though they belonged?"

But soldiers belong to the army. You only need to watch one military close-order drill to be impressed by the rows and columns of soldiers walking heel-to-tow in perfect order as though they were knitted into the same seam, if that is a correct use of the sewing terms. Marching is just one example of how the army trains its people to work together.

If you have never had to march in a large group, you might not appreciate how difficult it is. Actually, it is astonishing when if you think about hundreds of people walking side by side, stacked fifty or a hundred rows deep, and they (usually) can march without stepping on one another's feet. There might be a few marching bands that have a similar degree of precision when they walk, but when it comes to filing down the rough edges from individual personalities and turning diverse people into parts of a whole and getting them to walk together, the U.S. Army is in a class by itself.[1]

The army's marching raises an interesting series of questions. If what the Army does with their recruits works for feet, can the same process work for minds? And is it possible that an entire society might get that kind of harmony from its citizens? Can Americans walk in the same direction without stepping on each other? Could the entire country become a cohesive unit without drafting everyone into the army and turning the entire country into soldiers? The answers are maybe, maybe, and maybe. And maybe!

A big reason for the Army's training success is because the Army has a capability that few other employers have, and that is total control over the employee's life. The recruits arrive in the army as a collection of diverse personalities and they realize very quickly that individualism is now a liability. Another old adage, this time Chinese, describes the successful army training philosophy; the *nail that sticks up the highest gets hammered the hardest.*

From their first day, recruits learn that there is only one way to do things and that is the army way. They learn the new approach not because it is the best, but because they don't have options. The army does not want innovation or creativity from its soldiers; they want and expect total and immediate obedience to orders. When recruits follow prescribed procedures, they receive rewards in the form of advancement, weekend passes, and lighter duty. Lighter duty in the army is a good thing.

Not incidentally, the army also has an effective punishment process for people who do not follow procedures or orders. The punishment is

---

1 To minimize reader outrage, I am not overlooking the Marines, the Navy, or even the Air Force; it is fair to say that all branches of the armed services are effective in training their new recruits to march.

not like the old, brown boot days of the army, when violations could result in lashes with a cat-o-nine tails. Today's army does not physically punish people anymore, at least not directly. It doesn't have to administer physical punishment because it has control over a system of sanctions that can make hell out of a soldier's life. The sanctions might be worse than the cat-o-nine tails. At least after you got the twenty lashes, you were done with the punishment.

Critics should be careful about going after the army's concept of punishment. Successful armies throughout history, and it would be impossible to mention a society that was proud of an unsuccessful army, were the ones with effective systems of rewards and punishments. Proper training with rewards and punishments means obedience and obedience produces successes on the battlefield. Success is, after all, what armies are for.

Most Americans though are not in the army, and fortunately or unfortunately, army sanctions are not generally available when citizens misbehave. Americans don't have to ask for weekend passes, they are not interested in having stripes on their shirt sleeves, and they do not have platoon leaders watching their every move for violations. Close-order drill, that impressive demonstration of army discipline, would be impossible for civilians. Americans have trouble standing in a straight line let alone marching in one.

If citizens are not in the army, what enforcement mechanisms does society have for behavior control? Society does not have behavioral sanctions that are anywhere near as effective as the army system. In what political conservatives might call the *good old days*, offenders of even minor societal regulations could be whipped, branded, tortured, or even burned at the stake. The Salem Witch Trials were certainly one of the saddest episodes in this country's search for an effective way of encouraging proper behavior. The offenders executed in Salem, some twenty-three adults and fifteen children, forty-one in all, not counting the dog, were guilty of nothing other than unacceptable behavior.

But the country does not burn people at the stake for unacceptable behavior any longer. There is, of course, the prospect of time in jail. But although the U.S. is a world leader in its incarceration rate, jail is not often used for minor infractions. For the less serious behavior infractions, our society uses social disapproval as a form of punishment. Unfortunately, perhaps, Americans today do not care as much about social disapproval as they once did. Even acts that would once induce shame generate no more reaction from the offenders than a simple shrug of the shoulders and an explanation that, " everyone does it."

We are back to that earlier question; what is a person supposed to do when someone tells them to "behave yourself?" It will probably not be surprising if I suggest that American society is currently in a state of uncertainty about proper behavior. Maybe we have always been in that kind of ambiguous state, somewhat uneasy with one another. After all, we went to different schools, literally and figuratively, and we have distinctly different ideas of what everyone is supposed to do.

If there are prevailing rules for acceptable social behavior, and that is questionable, but if there are such rules, they are vague, inconsistent, and transitory. It is no surprise that children are confused about how to behave. Their parents are confused too. Americans don't always follow the same rules, and if they do, it may not be at the same time. Instead of precision drilling, we are running into one another, stepping on each other's feet with depressing regularity.

Even though our social interactions work fairly well most of the time, problems do occur. Sometimes the problems are almost comical, as when neighbors disagree about the proper length of front yard grass. There are also tragedies growing out of the disagreements. But the problems, the unrest, the occasional friction, and even the occasional tragedies might not be as bad as the alternatives. Close-order drills may look nice on parade days, but do Americans really want military precision in their daily lives if that precision requires the imposition of a rigid system of rewards and punishments administered from an absolute authority?

It does not require sociology training to see that many Americans are not in step with their peers. Some Americans will never be in step. A few individuals, maybe more than a few, do not like the routine of modern jobs and they look for alternatives. Some Americans enjoy rock concerts more than church socials, and others consider body jewelry more attractive than Rolex watches. And the variety of contemporary marital arrangements staggers even the modern mind.

But American society is not an army, and not everyone has to be in the parade. We should be very careful about our admiration for army-like discipline. An army's close order drills are not real life, and real life is not an army parade. I think we should be happy that we can still understand and appreciate the difference.

CHAPTER 5

Why Do You Think They Call It "Dope?"

• • •

FOR MORE YEARS THAN THE government likes to admit, the United States has been waging its "War on Drugs. " But individuals campaigning for re-election to political office and administrators testifying at law enforcement budget reviews are about the only ones carrying good news about the battles. And that good news is depressingly similar year after year; major drug ring broken by DEA agents; local farmer arrested for growing marijuana; fourteen people arrested in large city drug sting; California grandmother indicted for selling marijuana brownies to cancer patients.

Despite the so-called victories, the war isn't going well. As of 2012, eighteen states and D.C. have laws authorizing medical marijuana. Colorado passed a bill legalizing the drug for recreational use. Other states will follow, especially when they notice the potential for new revenue. It is still not clear how the federal government will handle the legal conflict.

If Americans evaluated the on-going drug battles they way they do the more traditional wars, the ones with uniforms, medals, foxholes, and *nested* reporters providing regular briefings from the front, they would be better informed about the drug war. And if they were better informed, it is likely that they would be demanding a negotiated peace. Or the country could, as one astute politician once suggested for the Vietnam situation and others now see as a good idea with the Afgan war; just declare ourselves the winner and get the hell out.

The problem with this drug conflict, or war if you prefer, is no one seems to know where *out* is. What direction is the country supposed to move in order to get out? Even after all this time and all that war, there is little agreement about who or what or even why we are fighting. And no one seems able to say how anyone will know when and if we won. This absence of clarity lies at the center of the country's dilemma with its drug war.

As with any policy issue, a little precision about basic terms goes a long way. Clarity also allows everyone to start from the same point, always a good idea whether the argument involves horseracing or policy discussions. We could make a good start toward this clarity if we can agree how to define the most fundamental term, *drugs.*

It would be difficult to think of a word conjuring up more unfavorable images within the public mind than *drugs.* Other than child molester, terrorist, or perhaps Enron executive, no labels are as reviled in this country as the ones centered in the drug trade; drug addict, drug lord, drug pusher, drug kingpin Americans tend to see them all as evil incarnate. The media support this pervasive negativism with their regular public service announcements detailing the evils of drugs. The commercial showing a hot skillet with eggs frying and the voice-over telling viewers that "this is your brain on drugs" is one of my favorites.

When Nancy Reagan started her personal anti-drug campaign many years ago, the catch phrase was "Just Say No!" (To drugs!) Like other sound bites, the phrase appealed to people because of its simplicity. Just say no! What could be simpler? As mentioned in an earlier chapter, Americans like simplicity. Unfortunately, Ms. Reagan never told her listeners which drugs they should decline.

If a doctor prescribes anti-biotics for her patient's flu symptoms, should the patient say "NO" to the drug? When a friend offers someone aspirin for a headache, or a pharmacist suggests a pill to lessen the effects of hay fever, should the sick individual say, "No thanks, I don't do drugs?" And what about drugs for pain, high blood pressure, depression, or even muscle stiffness? Such questions sound academic, and they are; but they are a necessary starting point for an understanding of the country's *drug problem.* We can't fight a war if we can't define the enemy. That lesson applies to other political issues as well, but that is a story for another time.

Anyway, despite Nancy's appealing message and the subsequent battle plans, the country hasn't been able to say no to drugs. America is a drug-consuming society, it has been for generations, and there is no reason to expect any real downturn in our collective desire to make our lives better through chemistry. Americans are consuming more drugs each year, billions of dollars worth, and the numbers are getting larger, not smaller. We take pills to gain weight and lose weight, we have pills for anxiety, for depression, for worries and for euphoria, and for just about any psychological disposition defined as a malady. If you have the symptoms, the pills will come.

One of the newer pills on the market is designed to cure Americans who have difficulty relating to other people. If you are uncomfortable around others, the commercials for the drug insist that the pill will help. The commercials seem to offer the possibility of a social recluse turning into the president of the local Community Welcome Wagon, a kind of social Cinderella. How can it get any better than solutions to complex psychological problems coming in a bottle? Small wonder there is this pervasive American proclivity for drugs.

One dictionary says that the word *drug* refers to ingredients that alter or affect the human body. This description is useful, but it is so vague that it can apply to every ingredient from cocaine to caffeine, and from marijuana to Mazola Oil. Some distinctions need to be made if we want to clarify the issues in the drug war. We are (presumably) not waging war on Mazola Oil, not yet anyway.

For one thing, we can distinguish the various drugs according to their consumer availability. Some compounds require the approval of a physician in the form of a prescription, while the over-the-counter substances (OTC) are available in drugstore aisles to any individual with the inclination and the money to make the purchase. Some professionals argue that prescription drugs are more potent than over-the-counter drugs and thus the need for physician approval. But drug users, if that is the right term, have died from overdosing on drugs from both prescription and OTC substances.

Consumers have also become addicted to drugs from both sources, so the notion of addiction potential is not a useful demarcation line either. But public officials still insist that prescription drugs in general have a higher degree of potency and so the government continues to regulate their distribution, presumably in the interest of citizen health and well being.

The idea of *public health* is another interesting element of the drug war. Who would argue against the public's health? Public health is one of the nation's common goals, one of the few things politicians seem able to agree upon. Although the nation's founders did not expressly use the term, they did emphasize the importance of the general welfare, and that concept sounds something like public health.

But however appealing it may be, that goal muddies when we ask questions about a particular drug and its potential effects on the public's health. If you want to start a computerized list of harmful drugs, you better have some memory room on your hard drive. You can start the list with tobacco and alcohol. No drug war with public health as one of its major goals can ignore the problems caused by tobacco and alcohol. Americans use, and abuse, the two drugs far more than any other drug, prescribed or OTC.

Tobacco and alcohol are available in the nations' retail establishments without the need for physician prescriptions. Other than the occasional admonition to "drink sensibly," or the printed health warnings on cigarette packages, there are no concerted governmental efforts to include tobacco and alcohol use as part of its "this is your brain on drugs" campaign. We will look further at this interesting inconsistency later.

But on the subject of legal drugs, there are other potentially unhealthy compounds available to the public besides tobacco and alcohol; Valium, Xanax, diet pills, sleeping pills, pep pills, and we should not forget caffeine, all these elements can and do cause significant and persistent physical problems. More than half of adult Americans, including me, are addicted to caffeine, a drug with its own set of health concerns.

Why isn't the federal government doing something about the caffeine addiction problem many of us have? If it is a good idea to design a sting operation on a California marijuana farm, couldn't the government mount a similar operation in a California Starbucks? What about the extra shots of espresso into your latte? That can't be good for you, not when we know how addictive caffeine is! Shouldn't a physician issue a prescription if you want to order a mocha java with five shots of espresso?

Let's not beat the argument to death. What Nancy Reagan and the rest of the federal officials had in their minds with the sadly ineffective campaign against drugs was that Americans should be saying "no" only to the drugs that the government considers inappropriate. The interesting thing is that the government's decision process lacks consistency. Tobacco usage is addictive and a major health problem, but if people choose to smoke, no one from Washington will stop them. The local rules may put smokers out of restaurants, and they would have to put out their cigars before getting on the elevator, but if they want to smoke, the government is not going to interfere. Not as long as there are American tobacco farmers who vote and make political contributions.

And the problems associated with alcohol consumption dwarf any other drug, including tobacco. Alcohol has a long and persistent trail of medical and psychological devastation for users. Alcohol use and abuse are associated with other social problems such as unemployment, degenerative and costly physical ailments, domestic violence, and of course, highway fatalities. If the public's health were the force in social policy idealists claim, alcohol would be available only by prescription. Take two martinis and call me in the morning!

It is fair to conclude that the government's toleration for potentially unhealthy compounds is somewhat selective. Americans need to grasp that crucial point if they want to understand the country's *drug problem*. The government picks and chooses the targets of its drug wars, and Americans should be asking their representatives, who is doing the picking? And why those particular selections?

Speaking of the selections, opium is an interesting compound for a discussion of the illegal drugs in the American marketplace. Although opium has been used medically for thousands of years, the plant is not an American farm product. This is not an incidental point. When immigrants from the east introduced opium to the United States a few generations ago, physicians regarded the drug as a dramatic improvement in their tools for dealing with physical ailments. Within a short time, many manufacturers included the drug in their retail products. The opium derivative, heroin, emerged in the late 1800's and this compound too was hailed by the medical profession as another *wonder drug.*

In the late 1800's, Dr. Fahrney's Teething Syrup had morphine and chloroform as ingredients. Dr. Moffitts Teething Compound had powdered opium. Although users of such products had the potential for developing a physical reliance on the medications, the medical community decided that addiction was not a problem as long as the individual had access to a ready supply. That is another interesting situation in the drug problem equation- access. And users did have this access, until the government decided that the public health was at risk. In the 1920's, opium and heroin joined the ranks of illegal substances and individuals could no longer get them. Not legally anyway. And then the problems with the compounds began.

Marijuana has a history almost as long as that of opium, but its use was permitted in the United States until later. In the early part of the 20th century, marijuana usage was concentrated in the arts communities, so it was mostly out of the sight and the minds of the general public and the government. An older man once told me during our discussion about life in an earlier era; "in the 1930's, if I was walking along the road with a bottle of gin and a bag of hemp, the cops would have arrested me for the gin. Now it is just the opposite."

Why are certain drugs illegal? The simplest answer to the legality question involves the existence of laws; when the government passes a law against the manufacture or use of a particular substance, the substance is illegal, and people who manufacture or use it are violating the law. They are criminals. Marijuana and cocaine are illegal drugs, at least at the federal level, and if you sell or use them, you have the chance of going to jail. Millions of Americans have.

This discussion on the nation's drug war is not intended to extoll the virtues of illegal substances. I am not supporting or suggesting their widespread use, and I stand alongside professionals who insist it would be in your best interests if you avoided the use of any drugs. For the most part, and keep in mind the word *most*, we are all better off physically and psychologically if we eliminate or minimize drug use.

But the point here is not whether heroin addiction is bad; it definitely is! But why the government elects to get involved with some substances and not others is of more than incidental interest. And the substances elected for illegality have less to do with public health than they do with economics, definitions of morality, and/or bureaucratic organization. Let's start with the last reason.

Government bureaucracies, like corporate bureaucracies, provide jobs for people. But government jobs, unlike most in the private sector, do not involve actual products that sit on shelves waiting for someone to purchase them. For government workers, the product, the item that determines how well they are doing their jobs, involves a service. The service in the case of drugs is the government's efforts in eradicating a substance that presumably constitutes a threat to the public's health. And we are back to the public health arena once again.

It is important to remember that the folks employed in the government's drug war are people who are performing their assigned jobs. Having jobs as drug enforcers, just as with meat cutters and mail carriers, means that the workers can buy food, watch television, and pay their mortgages. If a change in laws removed the need for professional drug enforcement, the change would also mean the elimination of the jobs that play the mortgages and buy that food. It sounds simple, and this component of the explanation for the continuing drug war is just that simple; a bureaucracy, government or private, is staffed by people doing their jobs.

Troy Duster, in his still relevant book, *The Legislation of Morality*, argued that making marijuana illegal was a bureaucratic rather than a medical decision. There wasn't much for drug enforcement employees to do once heroin use declined in the United States, so that governmental agency needed a new drug to make war against. Marijuana was a good choice because no influential individuals or organizations were involved in either making it or using it. The war on drugs, among other things, means jobs. When we consider the scope of the war, we are talking about a lot of jobs.

There is also a political advantage in having a national "drug problem." Drugs provide a political issue without a down side. Political candidates can campaign against drugs without alienating any significant voter block, other than users and sellers, few of whom vote anyway. The always abrasive climate in Washington would become even more interesting if the illegal drug trade had the same number of paid Washington lobbyists as the tobacco, alcohol, or drug companies.

It is also interesting to look at the types of people getting caught in the country's drug nets. The money flowing through the country's social and economic structures from illegal drugs is on the order of a flood, and it is difficult to find anyone in its path who has not gotten wet. But some people manage to stay dryer than others.

I don't want to construct a picture of completely innocent people whose only crime was the occasional use of an illegal substance. Some of the people in this complex picture are distinctly unappealing; the so-called "drug lords," for example, the sinister entrepreneurs who cannot find enough places to store their soiled funds. Or the officials of the off-shore and onshore banks that knowingly accept deposits of drug funds, serving as a kind of financial clearinghouse.

We have to include in this unpleasant picture the law enforcement officials who take money and allow neighborhood drug trading, even to children, to proceed with the classic wink and a nod. But most of the people at or near the top of the drug pyramid do not get their own hands dirty because they seldom get entangled in the enforcement nets. The ones who get caught in all the stings are the so-called mules who carry drugs across the border, the people selling drugs on the corners, and of course the addicts themselves, easily the most convenient targets.

No overview of the factors underlying drug illegality is complete without talking about the role of morality and the people sociologist Howard Becker described as "moral entrepreneurs." The entrepreneurs are the influential individuals who help to create and enforce social standards. They are not always public officials, although a public platform is useful for such activities. The moral leaders are the people who know what is right. They refuse to be influenced by factors such as cultural change or scientific data.

St. Augustine could serve as a good historical example of a moral entrepreneur. Fifteen hundred years ago, Augustine established rules about human sexuality that still ripple through western society. *Ecce unde*, he wrote; "that's the place," pointing to human genitalia as the locus for the evils besetting human society. (Augustine might have a problem sitting across the table from Hugh Hefner, but the discussion would be fascinating.)

This brief overview outlined the strong influence that laws, economics, bureaucracies, and moral entrepreneurs have on America's drug war. We come back to our starting point, the war, and the question of how we are doing. The drug battles support a massive workforce ranging from undercover agents to prison guards, all of them fighting mostly American citizens whose crime was producing, selling, or using substances the government says they should not possess or use.

There are thousands of cases of citizens being prosecuted and losing everything they owned because of their involvement with illegal drugs. More than half of the more than two million Americans currently in jail are there as a result of illegal drugs, and the national government isn't retreating without a fight; federal officials are currently attempting to prosecute California physicians who are approving marijuana use for their patients. There is a California state law approving the procedure, but that hasn't stopped federal prosecutors. It is too early to tell what is going to happen with Colorado's recent approval of recreational marijuana use.

There are people getting caught in the drug war who are not Americans. Their stories are equally compelling. For example, the farmers in the Far East who raise poppies, the raw material for many illegal drugs, are a major part of the world's opium supply. But not many Americans would consider the poor farmers in Afghanistan as enemies; the farmers raise poppies because the crops are the best way to provide enough income to feed their families.

What about the Mexican man who is trying to finance his family's move to the United States by carrying a few pounds of marijuana over the border? Does it make sense to put him in jail for twenty years? How about the Chicago woman hooked on crack cocaine and stealing CD's to support her habit? Should the nation's drug war machine be aimed at her? What about the college students purchasing a few envelopes of cocaine to add spice to their fraternity party? Should they be classed as felons for the rest of their lives?

It bears repeating that many illegal drugs are undesirable or have dubious effectiveness. Drugs that affect the human body should be studied and used carefully and with full realization of their potential short and long-term harmful effects. No reasonable person would dispute that assertion. But the nation's experiments with regulation on substance use have not always been successful. Prohibition, the classic example of government's intervention in the public's consumption habits, failed not because alcohol is a wonder drug; prohibition failed because Americans wanted to continue drinking. Alcohol has and continues to satisfy some of people's psychological and social needs. The needs do not disappear because the federal government passes a law.

When the government declared alcohol illegal, as one bar owner reported, "we just moved our operation from the first floor into the basement." And for the next decade, while government agents like the infamous Eliot Ness chased bootleggers through the streets, a new criminal enterprise grew and prospered. There is a parallel here with the current drug war. Drugs cannot be easily controlled; newer and even more dangerous drugs can even be concocted in basements.

Marijuana can be grown almost anywhere, and unless we are also prepared to outlaw sun lamps, some Americans will continue to harvest the plants in their basements and workshops. And as far as availability is concerned, one teenager recently said in a newspaper article; "it is easier to get marijuana today than it is to get a six-pack of beer."

It is difficult to accept the idea of *losing* the drug war, but it is hard only if we insist on using that pejorative term. We are not really losing anything. The idea that strict enforcement would end does not mean that the war against drug abuse is lost. The government would not be saying that the use of any addictive or harmful substance was a good thing; they would be saying that the government was no longer going to wage war on its own citizens.

Legalization of drugs, and this is what we are discussing here, does not mean encouragement. It means that if Americans want to use substances in the privacy of their homes, whether it is cocaine or crème de cocoa, marijuana or Miller Genuine Draft, the use is an individual decision. How many times can we say it? Many drugs are detrimental to the individual's health. But as long as the people using such drugs stay off the roads and away from their jobs, if the jobs involve public safety, that drug use represents no threat or danger to anyone but the user. Whatever restrictions the government might elect to establish could be done through the tax system. Five dollars for a package of cigarettes, for example, is a far greater deterrent to tobacco use than a whole squad of heavily armed DEA agents.

Unfortunately, at least from my perspective, legalization of drugs such as marijuana and cocaine is not on the political horizon. The courage required to lead this change in values is rare in the American political arena. Bill Clinton supported reduced penalties for drug use, but his support came on his last day in office. Many academics speak out in favor of legalization, but no one listens to them. And of course not many currently serving public officials are interested in getting involved in this hot button issue.

Legalizing all currently illegal drugs might work and it might not. We don't know, although it is difficult to conceive of a policy that would be worse than what we have right now. We are putting more Americans in jail, we are establishing increasingly intrusive police procedures, and we are destroying thousands of lives, in part because the drug war continues to serve the interests of influential individuals and organizations rather than public health.

Good or bad, right or wrong, effective or ineffective, it doesn't seem to matter; we should not look for a significant change in national drug policy anytime soon. As Nancy Reagan herself might have said; "Why do you think they call it 'dope?"

CHAPTER 6

So is Your Mother!

● ● ●

DURING WHAT EXPERTS CALL OUR *formative years*, our little friends would stand on the playground and spew hateful names or accusations at their classmates. Most of us, of course, never did any such thing.

The often- silly accusations range from the relatively harmless *scardy cat* or *cry baby* to potentially more damaging terms. Sticks and stones will break my bones, but names will never hurt me goes the classic retort, but any child unfortunate enough to get tagged with a label knows very well that the names can hurt. If the labels somehow stick to the individual throughout his life, which they sometimes do, the names can be devastating. In the current ere of the pervasive social media, this name-calling, and its effects, can be even more immediate, long lasting, and destructive.

There are children who acquire scars from the assaults that last for a lifetime. I met a man when he was sixty, and he could still be driven to anger if someone made the mistake of referring to him with a nickname he acquired in childhood. Sociologists don't use the term *name-calling* to describe this situation because it is not sufficiently scientific. They like the more impressive word *label* to designate what kids refer to as name-calling.

Label though is a sterile term. It doesn't capture the potentially destructive implications of the process. When people hear the term "label," they may think of the printing on cans of soup or on rolls of toilet paper. If social scientists wanted a more descriptive word to describe the name-calling, they could use terms like *marking* or even *branding;* such terms would conjure up more appropriate visions.

But it still makes sense, for consistency if no other reason, to use *labeling* when we talk about the name-calling process in the adult world. Careful readers will understand that *label* as used in the discussion refers to people and not cereal boxes. It is worth mentioning that we pay more attention to people labels than to the ones on boxes, although food labels are far more informative and certainly more objective.

As with foods, people labels can be positive or negative, but you never hear anyone complain about a positive label. If the cereal label says that it provides 100% of your daily calcium needs, who wouldn't brag about that? And on the people side, if someone calls you a doctor, an architect, or a television star, you are likely to be pleased about the label whether it is accurate or not. Who would not want to be known as a rocket scientist, whatever that is? It is the negative labels that hurt; who wants to be typed as a car thief, a tobacco scientist, or a pornographer?

Let's use a more popular example, if that is the right word, and look at the images that the label ex-*convict* raises. To clarify what might be an obvious point, but you can never be sure what is obvious, an ex-convict is an individual who has been in jail. Either you were in jail or you were not. If you stop to think about it, and you should, being in jail is a broad category.

For most of us, if a person has been in jail, we conclude that the individual has anti-social tendencies presumably common to ex-convicts. This kind of person, this ex-convict, cannot be trusted to live alongside normal people, the church-going citizens who pay their taxes, buy Girl Scout Cookies, and leave the tags on their pillows and mattresses.

After society tags him as an ex-convict, it doesn't matter if he is a car thief, a bank robber, a drunk driver, or a shoplifter, and it won't matter if the jail sentence was the result of conscience rather than greed. The ex-convict tag applies across the board to everyone who has been in jail; think about the idea that the term encompasses individuals from Mohandas Gandhi to Al Capone, and it includes Dr. Martin Luther King, Jr. Dr. Sam Shepherd, Martha Stewart, and, a host of former politicians. Ex-convict then is one broad label.

Former mental patient is another negative label. If you have this tag on your shirt, you are going to encounter problems and personal obstacles that have no relationship to whatever mental conditions you may have or may once have had. The country had a vice-presidential candidate a generation ago who came to realize just how detrimental it was to a person's professional life if he or she was ever treated for mental disorders.

The term "former mental patient" includes everyone from an individual who spent ten years in a state mental facility to the person who went to a psychologist for help in dealing with a mild depression. If you have trouble accepting how difficult life is for people who wear the label, imagine how the residents in a typical American neighborhood, how your neighbors might react if a *former mental patient* moved into one of the homes on the block or, god forbid, if city officials turned one of the neighborhood buildings into a half-way house for former mental patients.

How would any of the former patients convince their neighbors that they were cured and there was no need for anyone to stand watch in case the people exhibited some bizarre behavior that would be a danger to everyone in the community?

One way of understanding the dilemma faced by former mental patients is to understand that we never use terms like "ex-pneumonia patient," or "a guy who had a bad cold last week." The uniquely sticky label on people with mental disorders implies, at least in many minds, that such people will never be completely cured.

How could anyone demonstrate that they were "cured" of a mental disorder? Has anyone thought about how difficult it would be to prove that you were sane? If you were mistakenly tagged as a formal mental patient, how would you convince your friends and neighbors that it was all a mistake and that you are now and have always been sane? Can you imagine what episodes, from block parties, or actions people saw taking place in your house through some open curtains, how these things might be discussed at your sanity hearing? What kinds of erratic behavior you demonstrated at the local Halloween parties might your neighbors and co-workers introduce as evidence that perhaps you were not playing with a full deck?

Years ago, a psychologist studying the difficulties in diagnosing *insanity* had a group of his students voluntarily commit themselves to local mental institutions. The students' assignments, once inside the various institutions, was to convince the staff that they were sane. There were no restrictions on technique; the students could do or say anything in order to get discharged, including telling the staff that "the whole thing was a class experiment and I do not belong in this hospital."

None of the more than twenty students managed to convince the various institutional staff that they were sane. Not one! One patient told a student that if he really wanted to get out, the first thing he had to do was to admit that he had been sick. Rosenhan, the supervising psychologist, concluded that society had no reliable means for distinguishing between sane and insane behavior.

The label of being "under treatment for some mental disorder" can be just as devastating and just as hard to remove even though the individual had never been institutionalized. Once you make an appointment with a psychologist, you are *in treatment* and the labeling process is underway. You now have the label of *a mental patient*, along with the associated negative connotations. It doesn't matter if you are going to the psychologist for something as simple as test anxiety or as potentially serious as depression for the death of a relative or pet. In the eyes of society, you are under the care of a psychologist. Even that psychologist will have some labels ready for you.

If you show up early for your therapy session, you would be showing evidence of an anxiety syndrome. If you show up late, you might have an avoidance syndrome. And if you managed to be on time every week, you are compulsive, maybe even anal-retentive. At least one of Murphy's laws applies in the arena of treatment for mental problems; you can't win!

If we think about it, which we don't often do, we engage in this labeling of other people's behavior even when it doesn't involve something as serious as mental problems or prison time. We still call each other names. Some readers will respond, "so what!" Civilization will not crumble because of a few negative terms. And so what if people acquire permanent negative labels? If the people are welfare recipients, drug addicts, or ex-convicts, why shouldn't other citizens be aware of their past behaviors? There is a truth in advertising law requiring manufacturers to indicate the nature of the cereal; aren't we just describing the contents of human boxes?

This interesting line of reasoning stands up only if we accept three equally dubious premises: First, that the labeled individual was actually guilty of the act or the accusation. It is worth remembering that many individuals are falsely labeled. But once someone applies that label, it is almost impossible to remove. Politicians understand that. I remember listening to the reaction of a friend who, after reading of the acquittal of a man accused of murder, said; "I don't care what the court says. Where there's smoke, there's fire. The guy is guilty of something!"

The second dubious premise is that the connotations of the label in question apply to everyone in that category. How accurate is this statement? Would anyone feel comfortable placing all ex-convicts in the same category? Is a paroled murderer in the same category as a tax avoider, and are both individuals the same as the guy who served six months for drunk driving? And does a habitual drunk driver deserve the same treatment as the guy who was pulled over after leaving his best friend's wedding?

Finally, you would have to accept the third premise, that individuals categorized or labeled deserve whatever negative reactions they are going to get. This is arguably the weakest of three weak premises. At what point do we consider that individuals, whatever their transgressions, have paid the appropriate price? When do individuals earn the right to begin new lives? Are we ever going to allow for *new beginnings* or fresh starts?

There are strong arguments that our society would be better off if it had no labeling process. But even if most people agreed, and they don't, changing the situation won't be easy. From the days of Hester Prynne and her scarlet letter, Americans have achieved considerable satisfaction from labeling society's transgressors. Name-callers are not always mean-spirited; sometimes they are only what we might describe as sloppy thinkers. Perhaps unfortunately, sloppy thinking is not a crime; if it were, most of our elected officials would be in jail.

But when sloppy thinking or mean-spirited assertions are common, we need to take a close look at ourselves, as individuals, and as a society. A depressing number of contemporary Americans lose jobs, friends, and the social support they have every right to expect. Not only are we ignoring the potential contributions of our fellow citizens, we are in danger of losing the humanity we presume to possess.

The social name-calling then is a problem. It has been a publicized problem, with periodic tragic episodes involving school children, but it is an adult problem as well. The sticky labels, some applied intentionally and others almost without any thinking, can do enormous damage. Still, with crime, domestic violence, and terrorism on our plates, there is a lot to worry about now. In that context, name-calling does not seem to be that big a deal. But it is.

Dr. Martin Luther King Jr. once expressed the hope that his children would be judged not by the color of their skin but by the content of their character. Wouldn't it be wonderful if every American could be judged that way?

CHAPTER 7

"Are You A Little Old For That?"

● ● ●

It doesn't take long! At least it doesn't seem long. Shortly after leaving our comfortable fetal environments, although I'm not convinced that any of us knows how comfortable our earliest environments really were, anyway sometimes even before we even have the chance to catch our breath, the counting starts. After we tell bystanders how long we have been out of the fetal sac, the well-meaning onlookers are convinced that they understand what we are doing or not doing, what we are thinking or not thinking, and what we have accomplished or not accomplished. The assessments based on our ages begin early; and sadly, they continue throughout our lives, right up to the final curtain.

"Your baby isn't smiling at me. She is almost a month old so she should be able to smile by now! I hope for your sake she isn't going to be slow."

"Are you still feeding him in a highchair at his age? Can't he sit up by himself? It might be a good idea for you to have someone check his spine"

"Little Jake is almost a year old, isn't he? Shouldn't he be walking by now? And he is so small for his age. What are you feeding him?"

The age-graded assessments become more frequent and more critical as the individual's years accumulate. "She is sixteen years old and she hasn't decided what she wants to do with her life? What is wrong with her? A girl should have some idea of what she wants to do with her life by the time she is sixteen!"

"He is still single? Do you think there might be something wrong? I mean, I don't want to be the first to say anything, but there is something strange when a man is still single at the age of thirty!"

"Jim, you are sixty years old now, way past the time for you to think about turning your job over to a younger person. We need someone who is going to be more enthusiastic about new ideas. Besides, at your age you should be thinking about golf and fishing, not about automobile designs. Working on new cars is a young man's game!"

"Sure you have some leg pain, Donna, but what do you expect? You are almost seventy years old now, and pain is inevitable."

Where or when did all the age-based assessments begin? And why? Human societies did not always function with the sometimes silly assessments. It is hard, for example, to imagine a group of young Neanderthals, whatever *young* was back then, sitting around their cave lamenting the fact that they were not allowed to hunt mastodons until they got older. "Maybe during the next warm cycle," the parents may have said, although there is no evidence that the Neanderthals even had a spoken language, certainly not one that included seasonal concepts. On the other hand, why not?

But as time passed, what we often describe as progress came, and with it came a way of measuring the passing of time. Calendars emerged to gauge the process, and after societies had their calendars, it was only a matter of time (I did not intend any play on words here!) before people began to record and anticipate the year's events. The passing of seasons, the best times for hunting and planting crops, the best season to move to another camp site, such events doubtlessly appeared in whatever schedules early societies used to plan their lives. Inevitably, since the arrival of a new member of the group was a special event, people began to record the individual birth days. And it is understandable why many people wanted to remember their own special day after the emergence of astrology, which has been traced back as far as 3000 BCE. (Before the Common Era.)

It was a small step from there to the point when someone started counting and assessing human life years. At first, it was probably an incidental process, providing people with an index people could use to gauge individual development. Recorded ages provided users with a ruler that would measure how long people had been around and, all other things being equal, how much longer they could expect to stay.

Once humans began using chronological age, it was only a matter of time (once again, no play on words!) before its use expanded. How could anyone argue against the convenience and precision of chronological age? You could add, subtract, and divide the figures, and use the numbers to generate interesting projections; ten year old children have lived twice as long as five year old children, so it seems reasonable to assume that the older kids would have twice the knowledge and skills. And as far as the ten-year-old children are concerned, it also seems fair to conclude that they should have similar skills. After all, they have lived the same amount of time!

Getting control of personal hygiene, we commonly describe the process as being "potty-trained," although I wish that we could devise a better term, anyway, whatever we call it, this process is arguably the first significant rite of passage based on age. We could describe that plateau as the toddler equivalent of a college degree; in some families, the potty event is cause for more celebration than will occur for any subsequent educational achievement. The celebration is understandable because this particular skill, if we can call it that, releases the family from duties that no one, even the most dedicated parent, would describe as satisfying.

Any delay the child shows in completing this rite can produce life-long problems. In general, early completion of the potty training is good, and late completion is bad. Being a little late might put a label of "slow" on the individual that could be erased by other accomplishments such as high reading scores. On the other hand, being very late with the training, and most of us know a few people who still had some difficulties with their plumbing at the ages of five, six, and even later, this degree of delay can generate permanent psychological scars. No one should minimize the importance of successful, and early, potty training. Nor should we minimize the potential harm of applying an artificial age standard to determine exactly when a child should have finished this process.

After individuals get through this initial, and as we said, sometimes-traumatic phase, they usually have two or three quiet years. This period is used for the acquisition of capabilities such as language and what are described, for reasons known only to psychologists, as basic motor skills. But overall, this time frame is a relatively peaceful psychological period. She may not understand it then, but the individual will need this interlude. She should enjoy herself with the icons of early childhood; Santa Claus, Easter Bunny and the tooth fairy, because the kinder fantasies will disappear as the more challenging parts of life's spool unwind.

We can describe the next segment of the individual's life as *an arena* because it has as many contests and competitions as a sports facility. The games begin with the individual's formal schooling. This is when the judgments really start flying. Everyone crossing the child's line of sight, relatives, neighbors, teachers, preachers, even people standing in the supermarket checkout line, will be willing to offer an opinion about the child's progress, or the lack of it.

"Has he started school? I don't want this to sound critical, but he seems a little slow in the way he handles books. My Jeffrey was reading third grade stories by the time he was five. "

"She doesn't play any musical instrument? At her age, every child should be playing some type of instrument. My niece Michelle is only eleven and you should hear her play the clarinet. We are hoping she will qualify for a college musical scholarship."

"My boy is eighteen years old! He is old enough to vote, old enough to die for his country if he chooses to go into the army, which he won't. but if he did, he should be able to have a few drinks in a bar with his father. What kind of world are we living in that a father and son can't get drunk together?"

Everyone seems to have a perspective about chronological age and what a certain age does or does not mean. And people rarely hesitate to express their viewpoints, misguided or not. Even the government has opinions, and though its official opinions might be just as poorly-grounded as the guy in the bowling alley who was lamenting his inability to get drunk with his son, the government has the advantage of being able to translate its ill-founded opinions into law.

Government at all levels can and does establish chronological points when it presumes its citizens are ready to drive a car, smoke cigarettes, get married, consume alcohol, or run for Congress, pretty much in that order. Throughout the social systems in society, from community centers to city halls and from small clubs to large corporations, Americans of every ilk use chronological age as the key to assessing their friends and associates. The key question is, do the judgments make sense?

The short answer is, not much! And now, no surprise, here comes the longer answer. There are instances when there could be a good reason for using age as a decision maker. Retirement is one process where chronological age might be useful; there is a need to evaluate eligibility for private and social retirement benefits. Otherwise, it is easy to imagine groups of recent high school graduates lined up at the social security benefits table, surfboards in hand. That was one good example, but I'm not sure we can find any others.

Who wants to argue that all eighteen year old Americans are ready to cast intelligent ballots? Does reaching the age of eighteen insure that individuals are spending the time to acquaint themselves with relevant information about issues and candidates?

Will every individual drive an automobile responsibly at the age of sixteen? Is anyone out there going to argue that every sixteen-year-old person fully understands his obligations when he gets behind the wheel?

Driving and voting are the more obvious examples of how chronological age might be misused as an index of capability. The less obvious deal more with perceptions than performance. Chronological age, for example, does not provide any accurate measure on characteristics such as intelligence or creativity. We know, or at least we know based on our current understanding, that individual capacities in such areas are not accurately measured by chronological age.

Is age related to learning? It is possible to find people who still prowl through public libraries at the age of eighty, ferreting out obscure facts for a speech or article, or just researching something to satisfy a personal curiosity. On the other side, we see individuals who lose interest in acquiring any new information from libraries or anywhere else right after they leave high school. There are people in the creative arts who do their finest work in the latter stages of their lives. Other artists lose whatever creativity they once had before they are thirty.

Employment is a major topic whenever people gather to discuss chronological age. And they do gather and discuss. Will employees be able to perform their jobs after they get older? That is the question people ask in such forums. Here is the best answer: I was tempted to say "the right answer," but that sounds presumptuous.

But there are many studies showing that chronological age has nothing to do with job performance, attendance, or morale. The same studies often show that older employees are the most productive people in the organization. Many employers report that their older workers are more reliable, more consistent in their performances, and produce more creative work. It makes you wonder why employers are not doing more to keep their older workers on the job.

Employers have not tried to retain their older workers in large part because of what social scientists refer to as *ageism*, a term credited to Robert Butler, the first Director of the Commission on Aging. What the concept obviously implies is that American society views aging in general and older people in particular in negative ways.

It is no exaggeration to say that the United States is a youth-oriented society. The signs of the emphasis on youth and the negativism about aging are seen in everything from television to contemporary birthday cards.

There are certainly downsides to getting older, and it would be pushing anyone's credulity to describe the effects as positive. Our bodies know we are getting older even if our minds don't want to admit it. Our muscular strength declines, our lung capacity diminishes, our kidneys are less efficient, eyesight and hearing decline, and our bones get brittle. No matter what their physical condition, men in their sixties are not in the starting lineups of major league baseball teams. That situation could change if league expansion continues.

There are also age-based changes in physical appearance. Again, it would be stretching things to describe such changes as improvements. The physical alterations are definitely not improvements when they occur in a society that puts such high values on physical appearance. We have *liver spots* on what was once unblemished skin, we are missing hair where we want it, and we are growing hair where it has no business being. Our posture is not as straight, and our skin texture looks like a punctured balloon. In the eyes of the younger segment of society, older people look like hell.

There might be somewhat of a balance in all the changes, as experience takes the place of vigor, and the facial lines of understanding replace the smooth unawareness of youth. But the equation cannot be balanced when social attitudes toward advanced age are negative. The value that most industrial societies, including the United States, place on youth is arguably the key contributing factor to this age mania.

America values youth in a way and to a degree not seen elsewhere in the world. It would be accurate to say that the country worships youth; youth implies enthusiasm, creativity, vitality, attractiveness, and openness to new ideas. Conversely, old age implies the loss of energy, rejection of new ideas, diminished learning capacities, and physical unattractiveness.

So it is not surprising that Americans do not like the idea of getting older. No matter what their age, Americans want to act young, dress young, and mostly look young. Once they get near or past the apparently magic plateau of age thirty, a person's age turns into a sensitive topic. Trying to get information on age has always been one of the more challenging research questions for social scientists. Americans would rather tell you how much money they make each year or how often they have illicit sex rather then say how old they are. When I asked a friend who was celebrating her thirty-fifth birthday how it felt to be middle-aged, it took her three days to calm down and about a month before she resumed speaking to me.

John Maynard Keynes provides an interesting summation about the frequently frustrating human aging process: "In the long run, we are all dead." His statement may provide some comfort to people who are getting older.

Then again, it may not.

CHAPTER 8

In God We Trust!

● ● ●

HUMAN BEHAVIOR OBVIOUSLY INTRIGUES SOCIAL scientists; it would have to intrigue them or they would get jobs involving actual work. But humans and their behavior are fascinating even to the non-scientists. The way people behave on elevators, their body language as they walk through shopping malls or as they stand around singles bars waiting for the right person, the facial expressions in dental waiting rooms, body jewelry, platform shoes, slot machines and fantasy football, what humans do that falls under the loose category of *normal behavior* fills a lot of bookshelves.

Unfortunately maybe, and with only a few exceptions, usually involving members of Congress, we never know for sure what human beings are going to do. That persistent unpredictability is arguably one of their more endearing qualities, because humans are not exactly overloaded with endearing qualities.

One group of social scientists, the psychologists, spends lots of their research time watching the antics of white mice. It is easy to understand the appeal of the little creatures (the mice, not the psychologists); put a bunch of mice in a pen, construct a maze, add a bell, a few electrical circuits and some food pellets, and you have the makings of a long and successful academic career that with luck might include a few appearances on Good Morning America.

Critics insist that this research, besides being unfair to the mice, does not answer questions about human behavior. After all, the skeptics insist, we could predict how anyone, even the members of Congress, might react if we dangled their food or in the latter's case, their campaign donations from strings. Overall though, the research is harmless, except to the mice's mental health, and it does keep the scientists from other mischief.

If pressed, psychologists generally admit that humans are not mice. Some of the differences between the species, size comes to mind right off the bat, are significant. For example, humans usually wear clothes, and they have some ability to communicate both orally and with the written word. Humans also have a degree of *choice* in their lives that most other species either lack or possess to only a limited degree. Choices, alternatives, options, however we choose to describe the capacity, contemporary humans have a relatively wide degree of control over many components of their lives, certainly more than any other species.

Humans can take the time to examine the nature of their world; they watch, they occasionally ask pointed questions, they read, discuss, debate, and at some point they interpret the information. Part of that interpretation phase includes a selection process where they retain some information and discard the rest. On occasion, they may take action because of what they saw or heard. They are making choices and establishing at least the illusion of some control over their lives.

This process of choosing occurs in a variety of arenas; political activity, economic pursuits, family patterns, and a category that many researchers find particularly fascinating, religious behavior. I cannot imagine another segment of human behavior that supplies stories that come anywhere close to the ones coming from the religious sphere. Exhausting group pilgrimages to obscure religious sites, hundreds of people sitting on hilltops waiting for the approaching apocalypse, individuals in the southwestern United States walking the streets flailing their backs with a cat-o-nine tails, asking God to help their home team get into the finals, this material is more captivating than a Tom Clancy novel. Even economists are not as interesting.

But religion is more than unusual behavior patterns. Religion is an important social institution, and it merits a close look from anyone interested in human behavior. Especially the world as it is currently, with religious zealotry from many quarters causing havoc around the globe. Religion and religious behavior cover a lot of ground, so a few basic definitions would be a good starting point.

If we define *religious activity* as any beliefs, actions or attitudes surrounding things people do not or cannot otherwise understand, in other words what people frequently describe as *the supernatural*, the definition covers considerable ground. And it should! But where did it begin, this human fascination with the supernatural?

The precise origins of this supernatural focus are, unfortunately, lost. During most of their early time on the planet, humans focused on survival activities. They hunted and gathered their food as best they could, then sat around their cold dark caves waiting for daylight so that they could hunt and gather enough to keep them going so that they could get back to the cave and start the process again. Their lives were demanding; there were no breaks around the coffee machine, no weekend excursions to exotic resorts, and it would be thousands of years before someone would come up with the notion of retirement and a move to a Florida condo.

It is too bad that our ancestors left no written record of their lives for us to ponder. Even a Neolithic Wall Street Journal or a primitive Fox news report, would be helpful. Instead, if we want a glimpse at what early human days were like, we have to look at scattered shards of old bones, some pottery, a few crude pictures on cave walls, and on rare occasions, skeletal fragments. When the intact remains of an early human were found in Iceland recently, even though the man lived considerably after the Neanderthal period, the tremors were audible throughout the scientific world.

The well preserved male, apparently in his early twenties, had been encased in ice for thousands of years. An unusual series of thaws brought his body to the surface where it attracted the attention of hikers. I should mention that this early human was not killed by weather or accident, but by an arrow from one of his peers. The *Ice Man* might be one of history's first documented, and as yet unsolved, homicides.

It is unlikely that there are going to be many ice men, or ice women, found, so scientists have no choice but to deduce, infer, and then speculate about what early humans thought, what they worried about, and what their dreams were, if they had dreams. Early humans probably had words or gestures referring to food, water, fire, cold, and hot, but it stretches credulity to imagine them dealing with abstract ideas about the universe, eternity, or some form of god.

Though it is hard to visualize a Neanderthal family sitting around the fire after dinner arguing about the meaning of life, it is reasonable to picture the individuals looking at the night sky with the countless stars, perhaps a comet or two, and wondering to one another about all that vastness, what it was, and where it was. Since they presumably had limited language skills, it would not have been easy to discuss such vague notions, if they had them. On a clear summer night, one cave person may have pointed to a shooting star and grunted what today we would describe as a question. Her companion might have smiled and said something like, "Gratu lakk heretictious, Thesaurus!" which might have meant, "How would I know what it was?"

Later in the back and forth string of human events, permanent settlements emerged and with them came some leisure time, at least for the lucky ones. With this time for contemplation, humans developed tools, more complex language, and they began to harness alternative energy sources that provided even more time for contemplation and creativity. It was at that point, perhaps some ten thousand years ago, that humans started speculating in considerably greater detail about their existence and how they fit into what, even back then, was a very large picture.

Genetically, at least, the people ten thousand years ago and even before were pretty close to us. We are their children and the only thing separating us, other than time, which physicists today insist is not that big a deal anyway, is our attitudes, our experiences, and our behavior. If someone stumbled across a frozen human embryo from earlier times, perhaps belonging to the murdered *Ice Man's* spouse, and the technology was available to implant that perfectly preserved and frozen embryo into a contemporary female, we could test this interesting assertion. This assumes of course, that the procedure would pass the current ethics tests, which it probably would not, unless former Enron executives and a few bankers were on the ethics review board.

But if it did happen, when the child was born, she would have a 21st century existence and personality. She would go to college, and maybe law school, get married, eventually get divorced, and then run for Congress. Although the individual might not be as tall as her contemporaries, and perhaps she would have body hair in a couple of undesirable locations, there would be little else to mark her as a test tube baby from ten thousand years ago.

Fantasies aside, it would be useful to have someone, or something, from that early period of human history because this is when religion, at least as we know it today, began. Religious thought began because, with the free time, humans were able to start thinking about basic questions for the first time; where did we come from? What are we doing here and how are we supposed to behave? And where do we go after death? Is there a *next life*?

The early religious thinkers came up with some surprisingly durable answers to such questions. They also dabbled in other areas such as the role of sex in human existence and which movies would be appropriate for the children. Their answers persisted either because the arguments were difficult to refute, because the writers were the first to offer any answers, or because the earliest thinkers somehow came up with the correct answers. I consider the latter possibility as the most remote.

It wasn't until the seventeenth century, a wink of time, geologically speaking, that science, the new kid on the block, started looking at some of the same questions. Scientists also started to scrutinize the earlier explanations. Scholars looked, they poked around some dusty corners, they read, dissected, and analyzed, and they sometimes, though not always, debated their findings.

Among other things, researchers looked at the stories surrounding historical figures such as Moses, Mohammed, and Jesus as well as the narratives about presumed miracles such as the parting of the Red Sea, pulling Lazarus back from the land of the already dead, Noah and the great flood, and of course, the resurrection of Jesus. They also spent time on some of the more interesting religious doctrines such as the virgin birth and Adam and Eve.

It should surprise no one that many of the theological stories and associated religious doctrine did not pass scholarly scrutiny. Some researchers, for example, explain the Red Sea story as a situation where Egyptian chariots got caught in the mud. Presumably the details of the story as told in The Torah got pumped up over time.

And Lazarus was presumably not dead, at least not in the way most people think of dead. He was simply in an unclean state as Jews during that time defined it. Even the notion of the virgin birth, a central Christian doctrine, has an "explanation;" it was the fashion in early days to explain the birth of a child either from rape or from sexual contact during prohibited periods as a "virgin birth."

Again, it was not surprising that scientific explanations raised red flags in the religious community. But even theologians were starting to realize that the scientific examinations and alternative interpretations of religious traditions are not challenging religion itself. It is fair to say that despite the periodic disputes, the two approaches to understanding human history, science and religion, are neither always nor inextricably opposed.

Theoretical physicists recently introduced the intriguing idea that there may well be an infinite number of *parallel universes* out there, existing alongside what we once, apparently incorrectly, referred to as *the universe*. The idea of travel between the zones is, according to the physicists, unlikely, no matter what may have happened on the Starship Enterprise. But the prospect of alternative universes would change whatever notion we have left about the *uniqueness of human beings*, especially if we could ever devise a way to test the idea or if we ever had visitors from the other planes.

In my estimation, it would not be a bad idea of we managed to lose our prevailing sense of uniqueness. The change might help to make humans more accepting of alternative explanations for their questions. It could also induce a little more humility, a trait that also seems to be in short supply within our species. Understanding the relatively minor place that the planet Earth occupies in the scheme of things might also help the humility quotient.

I mentioned the friction between science and religion, but the theological friction points are not just between science and religion. Friction occurs with equal frequency, and occasionally with even more intensity, between the various religions. And there can also be friction even within the same religious bodies when supporters congregate to discuss and debate doctrine. Religious doctrine is more sensitive than a warm soufflé and it might be easier to alter the configuration of a mountain range than a long-standing religious conviction.

Organized religions provide their members with a conviction that they have a special status both in this world and the next one. True believers are special people, and their heavenly rewards are assured if they conform to doctrine and believe what they are told. Religious doctrine, the structure and content of religious beliefs, is then vital. And since that doctrine presumably comes from the highest possible source, change in that doctrine is not easy to come by. How often, after all, does God change Her mind?

This exclusive religious perspective does not encourage tolerance for other approaches. Researchers occasionally debate whether this religious exclusivity is good for the general society, but the debates are irrelevant. Whatever its pluses or minuses, its good or bad points, what it does for or against a society, this *religious exclusivity* is a recognized part of successful (i.e. growing) religious institutions.

Membership in a religious organization is not like buying a new car. Although both products, if I can use that term, have sales forces, buyer incentives, and provide numerous choices for the consumers, the selection is a little more emotional when people make a decision about religion. When consumers buy a new automobile, they chose whatever color, accessories, and style they want. And unless they bought a vehicle that went through the assembly line on a Friday afternoon, they have a car that will get them from home to work and back again with reasonable reliability and comfort. They might wish later that they selected a black car rather than the new shade of green that looks silly in the driveway, or that they had purchased the sports option that included a sunroof. But whatever they bought, they have the thrills, the smells, and the payments of a new car.

But there is a different purchasing process when people go shopping for a religion. They shop, at least in the broad sense of the term, but there is not much of a *comfort zone*, where consumers can tell themselves that one religion is much the same as the other. Unlike a car, consumers are playing for high stakes here, the highest! How can the stakes be higher than *all eternity* (although there seems to be a bit of redundancy in there)? Bad choices with a religion don't mean more trips to the repair shop, unless *hell* can be called a repair shop. And maybe it is.

As long as we are on the topic, the concept of hell is an interesting religious doctrine. Hell is the place some religions presume to send consumers who made the wrong choices, read the wrong books, or ate the wrong food at the wrong time. Hell is the ultimate bad neighborhood, a place described by one theologian as the spot where mad dogs and flames tear at your flesh for all eternity, where you suck the venom of vipers and where pain is your constant companion. Woody Allen provided another perspective when he defined hell as several hours locked in a room with an insurance salesman.

With such high stakes, people understandably think very carefully about religious choices. Although a few religions, most recently the Church of England, have abandoned hell as a doctrine, the more successful denominations still find the idea of mad dogs and viper venom to be useful recruiting devices.

Despite the high stakes, or maybe because of them, religious pluralism flourishes in the United States. The founding fathers would beam with pride over this pluralism because, political claims notwithstanding, it is just what they wanted. The country has a system, at least for the time being, that insures against any one religion gaining too strong a voice in the nation's affairs. American religion is not a single voice; it is more like a chorus. Maybe chorus is not the right term, since there is not a great deal of harmony when the organizations sing. In fact, harmony is relatively rare in the American religious chorus.

One uniquely American religious voice belongs to the Jehovah's Witnesses group, one of the more interesting, and discordant, voices in that national religious chorus. The Witnesses are not shy about proclaiming the superiority of their faith when they knock on your door. The Witnesses consider other religions to be creations of the devil. They call their own houses of worship "kingdom halls" rather than churches to distinguish them from the other, presumably heretical, places of worship.

The country also has *Apocalypticists* in its religious chorus, and they aren't exactly singing the same tune either. This group includes all the people and organizations that see the end of the world as imminent. They come in all shapes and denominations, and if asked, sometimes even if not asked, they point to physical signs like volcanic eruptions, heavy rains, or no rains, to support their claim that the end is near. The group seemed disappointed when one of their marquee dates, the year 2000, aka "Y2K," came and went without any major geological upheaval. Unless you count the Arizona Diamondbacks winning the 2001 World Series.

Psychiana is a classic American religious success story even though most Americans have never heard of it; the organization did not survive the death of its founder. Psychiana was a mail order religion started in the 1920's and based, of course, in Idaho, a state that grows fringe groups as well as it does potatoes. Frank Robinson, the creator, if I can use that term, of Psychiana, used newspapers ads and billboards to tell the public that membership in his organization guaranteed access to the Almighty: "I talked with God, actually and literally. And so can you!" It was the 1920's equivalent of, "You may have already won one million dollars!"

If you list religious success stories in the United States, and I suppose this is what I was doing, you have to include the Mormon Church. From humble beginnings, when Mormons were ranked alongside devil worshippers in the eyes of the other religious groups, the Mormon Church has moved to respectability. The church now includes governors, senators, presidential candidates, NFL quarterbacks, pop singers and actors as members, and they are, because of an effective, and unpaid group of young missionaries, one of the world's fastest growing religions. Although there are more than two thousand distinct religions in America, few are as successful as the Mormons.

The American religious market is not as large as you might guess, assuming that you guess about such things. One reason is the relatively low church attendance in the country. I mentioned in a previous chapter that most Americans do not attend church regularly. A recent survey on church attendance indicated that about one-third of adult Americans are regular churchgoers. Another way of looking at the situation is to say that two-thirds of the country is doing something else other than going to church on Sunday mornings. What else could they be doing on Sunday morning? (This was, of course, a rhetorical question; we know what kinds of options there are for Sunday mornings.)

Changing lifestyles are an answer. Life moves at a faster pace than it did a few generations ago. A hundred years ago, many Americans regarded an hour in church as a welcome respite from the workweek. Today, people look at that required hour as an irritating interruption. They are too tired or too busy to make room in their schedules for what they often see as just *another meeting.*

Things were much different for their grandparents. Long ago, there was always reason to go to church. Besides relaxation and socialization, there were answers to be found in the hallowed halls. The minister had explanations for, among other things, natural disasters; if there was a drought or a deluge that threatened homes and crops, there were answers in church. On occasion, the church provided the prospect of a remedy. There were prayers for everything from locusts to early frosts.

The religious explanations are now considered charming but usually irrelevant memories. To most Americans, a drought is a meteorological not a theological issue and a volcanic eruption has its origins from below not from above. There has been a similar evolution in dealing with questions about human eruptions. People today look to psychiatrists rather than exorcists to explain strange behavior by their neighbors and family members. And not incidentally, religious heresy, with the possible exception of Islam, is no longer a fearsome accusation.

It is no longer intimidating to challenge religious authorities. In a recent newspaper article on gay marriage, the writer stated that the Vatican had issued a *severe* document that proclaimed the Vatican's strong opposition to both gay marriages and to the adoption of children by gay couples. The Catholic Church went so far as to term the latter policy *gravely immoral.* The church went even further and insisted that Catholic legislators in various countries abide by its ruling and vote accordingly.

Since the Catholic Church is not well versed in democratic processes, we can forgive its presumption about issuing directives to elected legislators who happen to be Catholic. But their opposition to evolving and changing national policies on a variety of social questions generates a friction with a large non-Catholic segment of society and some resentment even within its own membership who think that there are issues about which the church should keep quiet.

The Vatican says that recognition of gay marriages would be an approval of *deviant behavior.* It uses that pejorative term far too loosely, unless of course the church means that most adoptive couples are not gay. We should remember that it was not long ago that the Catholic Church was equally vehement about discouraging deviant marriages between Catholics and non-Catholics. The Catholic Church, and this is true with more than a few religious organizations, has yet come to terms with the idea that values which seemed to make sense five hundred years ago are not longer sensible or even acceptable.

Societies develop rules and policies about marriage as they do with other forms of social behavior. Indentured servitude, for example, may have made cultural or economic sense at one time. It obviously does not make sense now, except when there is a need for cheap designer athletic shoes. A variety of social patterns that were good fits in agrarian, largely uneducated societies become poor fits for educated, industrial societies.

Religious organizations that remain closely tied to traditional beliefs foster this friction mentioned earlier, and are fighting a loosing battle against the needs of a modern society.

But this friction with social policies, with secular governments, or with one another, does not mean that organized religion will disappear from the social spectrum. People still want to know about God; is She out there, watching what people do, taking note when a bird falls to earth? Does She get upset when humans watch certain movies? How does She feel about dinosaurs, abortions, and Harry Potter? Are angels real? Is there some master plan for human lives, and will people who live their lives in accordance with the master plans reap rewards in the hereafter? Will non-believers be chewed by rabid dogs and be forced to drink their water from the heads of adders? No one, other than religious leaders and a few members of Congress, tries to answer such queries.

Another arena for religious growth, and what may be religion's most productive niche in modern society, is its counseling expertise. They may not have Ph.D.'s in Psychology, but religious practitioners are uniquely equipped to provide solace about the unhappy events that are part of the human existence.

When circumstances force people to confront sudden death, serious illnesses, or tragic accidents, it helps to have explanations for what otherwise might seem events beyond understanding. The frightening randomness of tragedies such as street shootings or plane crashes, where victims were simply in the wrong place at the wrong time, can devastate friends and family members. Secular explanations, that such events are part of modern life, are not much comfort. People will insist that there has to be a reason for the tragedy. Life, they will insist, is more than a series of random events; otherwise, why bother?

Such are the times when theological interpretations appeal even to the normally skeptical. Although research has largely invalidated the old adage, *there are no atheists in foxholes*, the notion that religion provides a unique source of comfort in especially difficult times is impossible to refute.

Religion also has other non-theological functions. Church membership provides a sense of belonging for individuals living in an increasingly impersonal society. Contemporary American communities often consist of people who are in one place only long enough to unpack the boxes. Indeed, many Americans spend a good part of their adult lives looking for boxes. With almost one-fourth of the population moving every year, America has become a nation on wheels.

Contemporary Americans live in transient communities, they work for employers who have little loyalty or sense of obligation to their workers, and the workers, not surprisingly, give little loyalty back. Like professional ball players and career politicians, Americans will quit their jobs today and pack their belongings if there is a better opportunity somewhere else. American homes are temporary shelters, no more than storage lockers for possessions until Americans gather their boxes and head for their next location.

More than forty million Americans move somewhere every year. Where do they go and what will they do after they arrive? But when they do get *there*, wherever *there* is, the loneliness can be overwhelming. Familiar locations are gone, and friendly faces are only memories. Where to go now, and who to see? The first place many individuals look for comfort in their new settings is the local church. That church represents stability and belonging in their unstable and transient worlds. Many churches as part of their services ask newcomers to stand up and introduce themselves.

As I mentioned, humans now have the luxury of time to reflect about their lives. They think, they listen, they hope and they pray. And after all their efforts over the generations, they have no better answers to life's basic questions than did their predecessors in the cold, dark caves of ten thousand years ago. It is possible that they never will.

Does it matter? I don't know; and I have never been sure that anyone else does either!

CHAPTER 9

Go Forth and Multiply!

● ● ●

It is interesting, and sometimes depressing to social scientists, that so few people talk about the world's population problems. Although population growth is arguably one of the most vital issues confronting the world, you won't get much information on the topic unless you read the periodic pronouncements of the U.N. Population Commission. Which of course almost no one does.

This aversion could be explained in part because Americans are "issued-out;" they are weary of pressing problems and impending disasters. What with wars, terrorists, energy prices, election speeches, and job insecurity, there is a lot on their minds now. So it is not surprising that the eyes of Americans glaze over when someone wants to talk about the world's population growth problem.

The notion that the world might have a "problem" with its human numbers is not a novel idea. You might even describe it as an old idea. Scholars as far back as Aristotle worried about population numbers. But in Aristotle's case, he was interested in a good number for constructing an ideal society. World population increases did not become a major topic for public discussion until the decade of the 1960's. But Americans talked about a lot of things during the 1960's. They were the heady days of war protests, boycotts, second-hand clothing, and the sing along music of Peter, Paul, and Mary whose classic song, *Puff the Magic Dragon* still raises the hairs on conservative American necks.

Some of the earlier population prognosticators concluded that our poor planet was doomed because it could not supply all the new arrivals with enough food, cars, or toilets, and in certain cases, not even the survival requirements of clean water and healthy air. There were people on the other side of the dispute, of course, and they insisted, usually with considerable vehemence, that suggestions about limits to the size of the human species went against fundamental, and to them non-debatable, ethical and religious principles. The distance between the two camps was too large for any workable compromise; not many people will move from where they stand unless they see a better destination.

"No movement" then describes where discussions on population policies have gone since the Peter, Paul, and Mary era. There has been some activity; in the 1970's, Washington politicians established a Presidential Commission to study the population issue. The commission issued a report that few people outside the academic world read and virtually no one supported because its recommendations for a national policy on population control went too far for some, and not nearly far enough for others.

In fairness to our elected officials, it would be suicidal if they took any position on population growth. There are few topics more likely to get them into hot water with their constituents, and there is no up side to the issue. There are no easy targets or villains. It is always more productive, career wise, to come out against drug lords, bad water, ineffective schools, or to favor something less controversial like government efficiency or a more sensible tax structure, whatever that may be. In the meantime, the planet continues to revolve and evolve, and the numbers of people standing around on the planet's surface waiting for flush toilets and hot water continue to increase.

Baring some miracle, which an earlier chapter on religion suggests is unlikely, the population increases and the accompanying problems will be with us for some time. Although the effects of the growth show up more often in the undeveloped countries, with the episodes of famine and violence affecting already desperate people, even the industrial states are forced to deal with growth-related problems. And although it would be reasonable to make a case that all social problems are "population related," because more people almost always makes a bad situation worse, it is still important, at least at the start, to separate population growth from other problems.

Population growth affects the world's ability to solve its other pressing issues such as poverty, environmental degradation, clean water, and affordable energy. More people makes solutions harder to achieve and always more expensive. But though it might make solutions more accessible, eliminating population growth will not by itself solve the other problems. In other words, if the world had a stable population size tomorrow, issues like poverty, bad water, and discrimination would still be there. This simple but essential point is often lost during the heated discussions on population growth. Keeping the distinction in mind helps introduce some clarity into the debates, and some clarity is never a bad thing.

Here are a few factoids about the world's population growth to illustrate the nature and scope of the problem. And that scope is enough to keep demographers awake at night, staring at their ceilings, with a sense that the sky is about to fall. Readers who are not fond of numbers or percentages may want to grit their teeth.

What we call the planet Earth currently has about seven billion occupants, give or take a few hundred million. Actually seven billion is conservative, although most of us have trouble visualizing even that number. Pointing out that seven billion people standing on one another's shoulders could reach beyond Mars won't help the level of understanding, because everyone will be thinking about the guys at the bottom of the stack.

The weakness and potential error with any number is that many undeveloped, and *poorer* would be a more appropriate term, countries have no accurate national census. So we are probably understating the total number by a considerable margin. But whether it is six, or seven, or ten billion people, we are talking about a lot of shoes walking the streets and lots of mouths consuming food and water. Seven billion people, and their fourteen billion feet, are doing their things, and meanwhile, the planet is adding more than one hundred *million people* to its crowded streets and dining room tables every year. Almost three million of the new arrivals each year are Americans.

All the new arrivals want a place at the planetary table, their share of the food, and of course, a car to drive. Especially if they are American. Although the world's population growth rate has declined in the last few years, and though there have been instances, mostly in Western European countries, where population numbers have actually declined, we should remember that this is overall a *declining rate of increase*. The planet's numbers are still increasing, although not as fast as some researchers thought they would. This is, I suppose, good news of a sort.

To get a better handle on the scope of the problem, let's look more closely at this world growth rate. It seems reasonable to use a one percent annual population growth rate for the planet; some countries are below that rate and a few, such as Italy, have reported negative rates of growth in recent years. But many poorer countries have growth rates in excess of three percent. It seems reasonable then to use the one percent figure to get some idea of what the futures holds for the planet.

As investment bankers can attest, a one percent growth rate means a *doubling time* of seventy-two years. In other words, with that annual growth rate, the world's population will double every seventy-two years. If we begin our projections in the year 2000, by the year 2072, the world would have 14 billion people looking for televisions, blue jeans, and cars to drive. In the year 2144, the earth would have 28 billion residents. This means more demands and needs. At least twice as many.

By the year 2216, and I can hear many readers saying to themselves, "who cares? I won't be around then." Anyway, by that time, and although you won't be around, presumably some of your descendants will be, there would be 56 billion people looking for enough work, water, and a place to park their SUV's.

This 56 billion population size for the planet is, of course, unlikely. Most researchers agree that the world is not going to arrive at that point because that size population is, by every reasoned analysis, beyond the planet's carrying capacity. The earth can only supply so much in the way of basic resources. There is not enough food, water, or even space to accommodate that crowd even if everyone moved into high-rises, ate smaller portions at dinner, and took public transportation to whatever work they could find.

So one of the few points of agreement among the groups debating the dynamics of population growth is that the growth is going to stop. The only questions being debated are when it will stop, and how. But it would be a mistake to minimize the importance of the two simple questions.

Thomas Malthus examined the world's population numbers more than a hundred years ago. He is considered a pioneer in the study of population trends. He would be shaking his head if he were alive today; so, for that matter, would the rest of us because he would be more than two hundred years old. After crunching the population numbers as much as anyone back then ever crunched numbers, Tom concluded that the world had a problem even back in the late 1800's. He concluded there was no option for solving the problem that did not involve human suffering.

Humans had no choice, Tom argued, but to let nature take its course. Based on the growth patterns he observed, he decided that the human tendency to procreate *excessively* meant human societies would periodically grow beyond their ability to provide for themselves. When human populations expanded to the point where the available resources could not support everyone, nature would step in with what Malthus, perhaps in a flash of gallows humor, described as "positive checks."

The positive checks meant that human society was periodically going to suffer from famine, pestilence, and war. The positive checks would reduce the population numbers until resources were again in balance. Then the sad but presumably inevitable process would begin again. Tom was not painting an especially appealing picture for humanity, but no one ever described him as an optimist.

Malthus did not, and he could not have anticipated the technological advances that have produced enormous gains in the world's food and energy production. So his central conclusion, that human populations would periodically outstrip their ability to provide for themselves, has often been inaccurate. But it would not be correct to dismiss his presentation entirely. Humans are still pushing the limits of the planet's resources. We are beginning, to use a farming metaphor, to *eat our seed corn.*

For the urban reader who may not appreciate that metaphor, any farmer can tell you that it makes sense, unless you have a feed store in the neighborhood, to keep enough seed to plant your crop the following year. You don't eat next year's seeds, even during a hard winter, not if you want to avoid starving every year thereafter.

The point is that we are not always integrating the prospect of *next year's crop* into our life styles. Humans, especially in industrial societies, have incredibly wasteful practices based on what seemed at one time to be unlimited resources. We know now what our ancestors did not know, that there is no such thing as an unlimited resource; over-fishing, energy depletion, devastated rain forests, species extinction, global warming, the concerns and crises are a common occurrence as humans continue to strip their planet's resources so that they can provide new arrivals with their needs. Malthus may be nodding his head and smiling, assuming that he is in a place where head nodding and smiling are possible.

Not many contemporary writers want to describe themselves as *Malthusians.* Who wants to be associated with positive checks? But as I mentioned, the people who have thought long and seriously about population dynamics, whatever they want to call themselves, agree that human population growth must eventually stop. And since that was one of Tom's central tenets, maybe they are all Malthusians.

If we start from this limited common ground, that population growth is going to end, we can focus whatever attention we have on how the world is going to get from here to there, from an annual growth rate of one percent to the point where the world's population is stable or even declining. It is worth mentioning that a "declining population' is not always bad. Anyway, it would be nice if there were easy answers; unfortunately, there are not. But some answers are more troubling than others

The desired stability in the world's population will occur when the number of people dying is equal to the number of people being born. There is a small caveat or speed bump to the process called *braking time* that has to be bridged before the world arrives at its stability point. In the interest of simplicity, and because I don't want readers skipping to the next chapter, we won't consider braking time.[2] Now that we have relegated the notion of braking time to a footnote, we can deal with the basic population growth equation, births minus deaths. The pluses in that equation have to equal the minuses in order to achieve world population stability.

This means that we have only two components that can be manipulated to produce this stability, births and deaths. Annual births have to equal the number of deaths. There can be some yearly variations, but over time, if we want population stability, there has to be equality in the two numbers. To achieve population stability, the world has to decide what it intends to do with one or both processes, how it wants to manipulate fertility or mortality rates. Or both!

Neither of the processes will be easy to deal with, but fertility is probably the easier of the two. If societies across the globe decide that they need to reduce their fertility rates, the goal would be for the birth rates to be at what demographers describe as the *replacement level*. The concept is easier to grasp when illustrated at the individual level.

When two people get married, for better or worse, the couple would have two children. They might chose to have less, but never more than two. With two offspring, individuals would be replacing themselves. If this replacement fertility level prevailed worldwide, it would lead to population stability and a zero population growth. It sounds fairly easy, but nothing involving human beings is ever easy. How does a society encourage or even insist on the two-child family? The answer is, very carefully! And not everything works the same in every society.

Most societies could begin the fertility reduction process by making safe, effective, and economical contraceptive devices as easy to obtain as aspirin. The fertility control devices could include the relatively new

---

2 Braking time refers to the time elapsed between the point when annual births equal deaths and when the population size actually stabilizes. The actual time difference, which could be as much as thirty-five years, depends on the proportion of the society's population that is under the age of fifteen. The higher that proportion of young people, the longer will be this braking time.

RU486 (or the morning after) pills, and while a society is at it, it might encourage development of a safe and effective male fertility pill. There is no reason for the finger of fertility responsibility to always point toward the female.

A limitation with the various contraceptive devices is motivation. The best birth control technology in the world is of no value unless people use it. The dramatic declines in birth rates in Western Europe that began in the early 1700's and continued for more than two centuries occurred without the availability of any modern birth control techniques. The key to contraceptive fertility reduction is that individuals must want to limit the sizes of their families; if the motivation is strong enough, people will seek out the most effective contraceptive devices. A contraceptive gel in ancient Egypt used crocodile dung as one of its primary ingredients, which will give you some idea of how far humans go when they want to limit the sizes of their families.

One of society's roles can be to consider what kinds of incentives they can or should provide to stimulate positive attitudes about smaller families. One possibility involves increasing educational and economic opportunities for women, especially in the poorer countries. Females across the world seem to recognize the relationship of family size with individual and family well being faster than males, and faster than the religious organizations that usually, and not incidentally, are dominated by males.

A few governments have tried to promote lower fertility rates, but the results have been mixed. Opposition to the programs was sometimes so strong that the fertility reduction programs disappeared. The Chinese government, which has more control over its citizens than many societies, has been more successful with their population reduction programs, but some argue that the effectiveness comes with too high a price. And that government has recently been relaxing its "one-child family" programs.

Economic incentives to limit fertility can be effective. Societies can promote lower fertility rates by eliminating tax deductions for additional children, establishing higher tax rates on larger families, imposing an educational tax on parents of primary school students, or introducing tax rebates for childless and one-child families. Such programs are possible and reasonably effective, and all of them are equally unlikely to be introduced, at least in the United States.

The problem with most fertility reduction policies then, is not with the number of options, but with the potential for intense objections. A high proportion of the world's citizens, and probably most Americans, oppose the idea of their governments getting involved with family size. When you add the voices of the various religious organizations, programs for planned fertility reduction can generate an almost insurmountable barrier to any fertility reduction program.

I mentioned religious opposition, and that point deserves elaboration. Organized religious groups can be the most effective opposition to any government's fertility programs. Some of the world's major religions, Catholicism, Islam, and the Latter Day Saints, for example, either forbid the use of artificial birth control or actively encourage large family sizes. Some cultures define a male's manhood, and a female's worthiness, by family size. Such values and practices are formidable opposition for any government that hopes to promote a voluntary and effective fertility control program.

Considering the persistent opposition to fertility control programs, it would be convenient if there were other options for reducing population growth. Migration was an option once. In earlier times, before Peter, Paul, and Mary started strumming their guitars, there were places for crowded countries to send their unneeded or excess residents. There were new worlds to explore and vacant lands to populate.

America was once the ideal New World. The excess citizens from other countries came to make their fortunes in a rich land, unpopulated except for the natives who no one counted anyway. The Irish came, the Italians came, the Chinese came, even some French came; the immigrants left countries that had problems and crowds and they headed for a place they thought more hospitable to their families, their lives and their dreams. They hoped for open doors and ample opportunities, and they generally, though not always, found such things.

But the world is different now. There are fewer open doors and fewer unrestricted opportunities. No country in the world today accepts unlimited numbers of immigrants and many countries including the United States are trying to find effective ways of discouraging new immigrants.

We are back to that equation and its two difficult components. If humans do not like the idea of encouraging lower fertility, there is only one other option and that is to work with the death rate. And who, other than good old Ebenezer Scrooge, wants to come out in favor of more death?[3] "Better they should die and decrease the world's surplus population," was Scrooge's approach, at least before Jacob Marley made his compelling presentation. As difficult as fertility reduction programs might be, the ethical and personal dilemmas accompanying any actions designed to increase mortality rates would make fertility reductions seem ridiculously easy.

American politicians often describe the country's Social Security Program as the third rail of American politics; touch it and you die. You could describe fertility or mortality control programs in the same way. People across the world, and Americans in particular, do not like the idea of their government getting involved in a decision as personal as family planning or the timing of one's demise. In an environmental attitude survey I conducted a few years ago, one respondent wrote a strong response to a question about the government getting involved in fertility rates; "No one is going to tell me how many kids I'm going to have." I wonder how she would have reacted if the survey contained a question concerning the government getting involved in stimulating mortality increases.

The population projections used at the beginning of this chapter stopped at the point where the world would be in about two hundred years. At that point in history, and this is only a few generations from now, a veritable wink of an eye, geologically speaking, the world would have a population of almost sixty billion people.

Assuming that the world could find the means to supply all the people with adequate food, shelter, clothing, automobiles and electrical

---

3 Readers who wondered about the book's title need wonder no longer.

appliances, and again assuming that the one percent growth rate contin-ued, then how high can or should the numbers go? There are two separate questions here, with the potential for distinctly different answers.

Do resources and their availability impose any limits to the size of the species? Is there some validity to old Tom Malthus' argument after all? And even if he was wrong and the world could find a way to feed and cloth an infinite number of residents, what would the quality of life be like with sixty billion residents on the planet?

If we have no reservations with sixty billion residents, what about a hundred? Or four hundred billion? It is surely appropriate to raise ques-tions about the effect the increased numbers of people would have on seg-ments of our lives that we don't spend much time thinking about, such as wildlife, open space, and recreational activities. Should we give the other items as much weight in the quality of our lives as we give to individual rights on family size?

There are lots of questions here and no easy answers. Readers who are interested in the projections though should take their pencils in hand, or more probably their calculators, because few people do long multiplication anymore.

Anyway, however you do it, go forth and multiply!

CHAPTER 10

Don't Drink The Water!

● ● ●

MONTEZUMA, A MAN WHOSE THIRST for revenge haunts international travelers, was the leader of the Aztecs when the Spaniards invaded that part of the world more than five hundred years ago. Montezuma made the fatal mistake of assuming that the Spanish leader, Cortez, was a god, a serious error in judgment that cost him his life and doomed the entire Aztec nation. Montezuma's posthumous revenge has plagued tourists for generations ever since, and not just Spaniards, although you have to wonder what vengeance Montezuma would have wanted from a Wisconsin family vacationing on a sunny Cancun beach.

Anyway, whenever Americans schedule trips out of the country, especially if it involves a sojourn south of the Rio Grande River, well-meaning friends will advise the potential travelers, "don't drink the water." If you think about it, and you should, this is an unusual bit of advice to give people who are packing bags for a long trip. What are the tourists supposed to do if they don't drink the local water? Not many people would be able to carry enough water for even a weekend's consumption.

Then there is the reaction of the local people to consider. When they see tourists pull out a personal water supply from a backpack, what are they going to think? "Your water might be good enough for you, but not for me," would be the message, and local people could take offense. *When in Rome, do as the Romans do,* is probably sounder advice for the traveler than any suggestion about bringing water from home, Montezuma and his revenge notwithstanding.

But overseas travelers are not the only ones who should worry about what is flowing from the local water tap! Americans are convinced, not without cause, that they have the safest drinking water in the world. They would be likely to insist that bad water was a problem elsewhere on the planet, probably in remote third-world villages where residents haul drinking water from the back of an old and usually dirty water truck.

We have seen the televised images. It is fascinating, to me anyway, how remote villagers carry their water back and forth in plastic milk jugs. Given the remote location of the places, you would expect their water containers to be ornate ceramic pots, large palm leaves, or perhaps goatskins. But old plastic milk jugs? Has anyone else wondered how the plastic jugs made their way to the remote villages? Is this what our national recycling program has accomplished?

Anyway, as Americans watch the water-hauling scenes, they probably dismiss the images as unfortunate episodes in faraway lands. If they continue thinking about it, they are happy that such things do not happen in the United States. American drinking water, and many citizens believe this, comes from special places; pure mountain streams perhaps, or flowing down from snow-covered mountains where people dip their cups into the clear blue water, drink deeply, and marvel at the wonder of nature's bounty. From the land of sky blue waters, as the old beer commercial song went, implying that beer made from the headwaters of the North Woods had to be good. And so, presumably is our drinking water.

But most of us don't know where our local water comes from. Every time I go on a trip, I make it a point to ask local residents, "by the way, where does your water come from?" I get strange looks and nine times out of ten, responses like; "where everyone else's comes from, I guess;" "now that you asked, I'm not really sure." Or "I just turn on the faucet and there it is. Why wouldn't it be?"

It is fair to say that most Americans take their water supply for granted. Water is water, one of the daily items we don't think much about, unless we live in the parched Southwest or the drought-prone areas of sunny California or sunny Florida. Or in Flint, Michigan, where the water supply there has turned into a major scandal that is causing considerable problems for the state's governor.

Who else worries about water? You turn on the faucet and there it is, running out in a cold and, you hope, colorless and odorless stream. Whether you are washing your clothes, your cars, your sidewalk or your body, the water you need is usually there. If the taste is a little strange or metallic, and many times it is, there is always bottled water. But you can use even smelly tap water to wash the sidewalks!

On the rare occasions when the faucet does not produce the water, Americans call the plumbers, the guys with vans that have the long pipes on the top. (I have not yet encountered a female plumber, and I have been looking!) If you have no water, the tradesmen can usually find the problem. Not many Americans have heard their plumber say, "I'm sorry, but there is nothing I can do. You are out of water. If you are interested, my company sells composting toilets."

No more water? This means no water for cooking, for washing clothes, washing sidewalks, or for making lemonade. Who in this bountiful country could even think about that possibility? If Americans contemplated their life without an adequate supply of safe water, they would realize what much of the world already knows, that the availability of healthy water is more than just a convenience. It is one of life's basic necessities and nothing to be taken for granted.

We know the role that water plays in the personal cleaning process. Dirty sidewalks or grimy driveways are one thing; it is hard to imagine how the quality of our lives would suffer if our clothes, our houses, and our bodies, could not be regularly washed. Lack of cleanliness may not be a fatal condition, but it would qualify as an unpleasant one. Confronting the sights and smells of human sweat and grime on a daily basis would be like living full-time in an NFL locker room, but without the showers.

Water is also a vital ingredient in nature's growth cycle. Humans don't often think of themselves as part of a natural cycle, but we are. And that vital cycle can be interrupted. If, for example, there is no water, there will be less food, and less food means that many people will not have enough to eat. A few individuals might insist that they could subsist on fast food chicken, but even the chickens need food and water. They may not get any sunlight, but they need that food and water. Every living thing has such requirements.

Humans also consume water directly and not just through chicken legs. There is nothing like a glass of cold water when you are desperately thirsty, when you don't have enough moisture in your mouth to even swallow. Everyone who has seen the movie, *Lawrence of Arabia*, can visualize what a persistent thirst might feel like. Although relatively few Americans have to walk around the Sahara Desert, they need an adequate supply of drinking water. Maybe not the eight glasses a day that a few experts recommend, but humans must drink enough to keep their bodies properly lubricated.

Water has another, perhaps less essential quality that is harder to quantify. Water has an aesthetic component, a quality that artists and poets have long recognized. But even non-poets know of the relaxing, even healing qualities of water. If we don't live near large bodies of water, we go in that direction every chance we get. Water, not power, is the ultimate aphrodisiac.

We cherish our moments sitting by a quiet lake, watching a meandering river, or wiggling our bare feet into the beach sand while watching the ocean. The majority of human beings live within a short distance of a major shoreline. Although much of this settlement stems from the basic needs provided by water, there is also a mystical element involved in the settlement patterns. Humans enjoy being around water; it is part of who and what we are.

When you consider its varied contributions, some essential and others merely desirable, it is unreasonable to dismiss concerns about water's availability and safety. The old cowboy movies often revolved around water rights; the bad guys had the water and wouldn't let the other people have any, not until the arrival of the good guy, usually played by John Wayne or Randolph Scott. Some politicians have not learned the lesson about water's essential importance yet. They will, as Michigan politicians might now be able to tell them.

How many Americans have a significant *water problem?* The answer depends on how we chose to define the term, "problem," and how we deal with the almost as slippery term, *significant.* Theoretically, and doesn't everyone love that term, there is plenty of water on the planet. It might be helpful to review some basics about the water we need so much.

The earth's water resources are a closed system, something like an automobile air conditioner, except that the earth does not leak and it doesn't have a tank to fill when it is low. The planet's water supply moves constantly; water in the lakes and oceans evaporates and this atmospheric moisture circulates, eventually falling where it replenishes lakes and streams and nourishes the green plants that feed the chickens in the dark warehouses. Not incidentally, plants also release moisture into the atmosphere as they grow, and this process makes another contribution to water's circulation cycles. Some of the rainwater seeps underground, where it sits until humans who do not live close to surface water pump it up to use for their lemonade, their hot showers and their car washes.

Wherever they get their water, from lakes, streams, or underground aquifers, after people are done drinking or washing, the *used water* goes back into the system and the cycle continues. Nature is a fairly efficient recycler. One researcher estimated that the average drop of water in the Mississippi River could be used more than twenty times on its journey from Minnesota to the Gulf of Mexico. This is why it is better to drink iced tea in Duluth than in New Orleans.

Nature's water system, like the plumbing in a well-built house, works pretty well. But early in their interesting history, humans decided that nature's hydrologic system had weaknesses and needed adjusting. Sometimes humans wanted *more power*, as television's Tim Allen used to say. Other times they didn't like the inconvenience of periodic flooding. So they made their corrections, and the results of the human tinkering were pretty much the same as when Tim made his mechanical adjustments.

Nature was never the same. Humans chopped trees, irrigated deserts, paved roads, drilled wells, drained wetlands, and flooded valleys, all in their ongoing effort to make nature's water supply more convenient or less intrusive. But we are beginning to understand that, as the old butter commercial said, *it's not nice to fool with Mother Nature.*

As if tinkering with the planet's plumbing wasn't bad enough, humans also abuse their water in a way that makes it hard for the guy who has to use it the next time. Ecologists would describe the scenario, at least for the secondary users, as living downstream. What humans do not always understand is that we all live downstream.

I always enjoyed watching student reactions the first time I explained that the water their neighbor flushes down the toilet tonight could be in their drinking glass next week. That illustration might be slightly exaggerated, but when you are teaching undergraduates, you make your points where and when you can. Besides, pure water is more of a marketing concept than a scientific one. It is fair to say that every drop of water we drink today has been used, probably many times, before it reached our glass.

The idea of used water should not cause anyone to panic or swear off water; it is not like acquiring a used car, when you don't know where it has been or who was driving it. There is nothing necessarily bad or unhealthy stemming from the re-use of water. Our planet recycles everything, and the process generally works pretty well. The problems come when the water is not properly cleaned of the contaminants that may have been inserted by previous consumers.

Some generations ago, people could say that a river cleaned itself every ten miles. And they did say it. But that was before a river like the Mississippi had to absorb the wastes from millions of people, boats, and businesses. Rivers today have a much harder time cleaning themselves.

The abuse humans foster on their rivers is not always due to large numbers of people. Modern societies use an incredible number of chemicals that, we are told, enhance the quality of our lives. Better things for better living through chemistry might be a good marketing phrase, but the practice has left residual ingredients such as PCB's, DDT, TCP, and a variety of other pesticides, herbicides, and fungicides in our water system. The discarded compounds do not always produce better living for everyone.

Environmental horror stories about the local water quality are depressingly common; lakes and rivers filled with fish too contaminated to eat, ecological dead zones in the Gulf of Mexico larger than some American states, warnings about contaminated municipal water, it seems rare for a week to go by without a story about some American water problems. Even animal waste, which in earlier years was a useful fertilizer, is now a major water pollution problem in areas that have factory farms.

Summing all this up, and it ain't easy, the nation's water supply is not in great shape. It is fair to predict that the water supply in many parts of the country will get worse before it gets better. The problems are so deep-seated and the solutions often so expensive sometimes it is hard to know just where to begin. Very often the problems belong to local governments that do not always have the funds needed to clean their water supplies.

Sometimes I think it would be a good idea to have the U-Haul organization take charge of the nation's water supply. They handle their rental business fairly well, and renting trucks is not much different from renting water. The U-Haul representatives will give you a truck in Chicago and you can drop it off in Los Angeles, assuming that you would want to go to Los Angeles. You can even drive the vehicle back to Chicago. The U-Haul organization is very flexible that way; as long as you return the truck with the gas tank topped off and no (new) dents, they will be satisfied and you will not pay additional charges, especially if you purchased the optional liability insurance for only a few extra dollars a day.

The key to their rental business approach is that the customer must return the equipment in the same or better condition as when he got it. If the U-Haul people took charge of renting the nation's water, they would take steps to guarantee that the water came back in the same or better condition. If the user returned the water in worse shape, with suspended particulate matter for example, or if it had some herbicides that the customer sprayed on his sidewalk cracks, the customer is going to pay extra for the required cleaning. After all, the company would say, they have to send the water out again and it has to be in good condition for the next person.

Unfortunately, there is no national or global water rental agent, and it is unlikely there will ever be one. So there is no one to insure that users are putting the water back in the same or better condition. It is not hard to imagine what that U-Haul rental fleet would look like if no one checked the condition of the vehicles as they came back onto the lot.

The next time you watch television and see a news clip of people lining up with plastic water jugs behind a dirty water truck, you might want to think about that situation becoming common in the United States. Because all of us, remote villages and New York residents, Chicago home owners and Wyoming ranchers, even the people who feel smug because they drink bottled water, we all drink from the same well.

Somewhere, Montezuma is smiling.

CHAPTER 11

"I'll have to check that with my supervisor!"

● ● ●

CAN ANY OF US THINK of a contemporary social institution that is as widely maligned as bureaucracies? Nothing else and no one else, with the possible exception of members of Congress, tobacco scientists, or Enron executives, generates as many bad reactions. The nation's business schools have classes and sometimes entire curricula to critically analyze bureaucracies, consumers blame the organizations for everything from high prices to shoddy educations, ambitious CEO's vow to change them, and generations of politicians have built careers on their campaign promises to reform them, abolish them, or at least reduce their influence. The rest of us, the few who did not fall into one of the preceding categories, worry about the corporate behemoths. Whatever our experiences, most of us share a fundamental misunderstanding of what a bureaucracy is, and what it does. And surprisingly, what it usually does pretty well.

Despite its persistently negative image, a bureaucracy is not the result of some massive economic inertia, and there is not an international plot to undermine the American way of life using bureaucracies as weapons of cultural destruction. Difficult though it may be, it is important to forget the invectives and the accusations and focus on one central fact; a bureaucracy is just another way for groups to organize so that they can accomplish vital tasks.

To put it another way, bureaucracies are a collective means for getting things done; that's all there is to their existence; no more, but no less either. This sterile description is less emotional and maybe a little less satisfying than the popular depiction of the bureaucracy as a collection of mean-spirited individuals out to make life miserable for everyone; but it is more accurate.

In earlier times, before industrialization changed everything, life seemed simpler. And it was. Human lives were not necessarily better back in the pre-industrial days, they were just simpler. And simpler sometimes seems better. There was a corresponding simplicity in business organizations. Direct communication between workers and owners was possible. Organizations were small; workers knew the boss and could talk to him personally about their problems and grievances. The talks probably didn't do the workers much good, but at least they had the satisfaction of the communication.

In the political world, voters, even the ones not living in Iowa or New Hampshire, could actually talk directly to politicians. Just over one hundred and fifty years ago, which is really not that long, President Abraham Lincoln reserved one morning each week so that constituents could talk to him personally about their problems and questions. Can anyone imagine the line outside the White House if that practice continued today?

But things have changed considerably in contemporary society, and this change includes the political arena, industry, and all the other activities that address the needs of a growing population. There are more people now, and they have more needs and issues. Supplying the needs and resolving the issues requires more efficient organizations than the ones serving the populations in pre-industrial days. We might not like the idea, but the early organizational structures with all that direct communication are gone now and they ain't coming back.

Several years ago, there was a small independent grocery store a few miles from the rural area where we lived. One of the large grocery chains announced their intention to build a new store just two blocks from this Mom and Pop operation that had been in the community for several generations. Regular customers from all over the area insisted that they were not going to change their buying habits and they would continue patronizing the old reliable store with its crowded aisles and sometimes fresh produce. The customers promised to ignore the existence of the outsider no matter how efficient its operation and how much cheaper and fresher the products. The people's intentions were probably sincere. But three months after the chain store opened, the Mom and Pop grocery closed.

The simpler organizations, with Mom or Pop walking the room with Christmas baskets for their workers, are disappearing. It is a sad fact that Mom and Pop, bless their hard-working hearts, cannot do the job as well as the larger, impersonal, and efficient organizations. Mom and Pop might be wonderful people, but their limited size means they are not as efficient in purchasing, processing, or selling products. And efficiency is the name of today's game, in groceries, clothing, and in most other items that comprise the needs of our daily lives. There are a few exceptions, like restaurants, but only a few.

If an organization has only a handful of employees, perhaps ten or twenty, it is reasonable to have all the workers hired by the owner and reporting to her. But as the organization grows, so do the demands on that owner's time. At some point in the growth cycle, it is no longer feasible for the owner to handle each hiring or to give every employee unlimited access. The owner will hire a personnel director, now referred to as the human resources director, and this new person will handle the contacts. Employees will begin to see the owner only at the annual Christmas party, if there is one, and if she isn't too busy to attend.

Eventually, if the organization continues to grow, the human resources director will hire specialists to handle issues such as medical care, retirement programs, and a motivational expert to address problems with excessive absences and poor employee attitudes stemming, at least in part, from the gulf employees feel now exists between them and the owner. Another bureaucracy has emerged.

The same process of organizational change and bureaucratic development occurs in both the public and private sectors, and the process happens in industrial and industrializing countries across the world. It is a basic management and production principle that as product and service demands increase, organizations grow and their internal structures adapt to meet the growth demands. Organizations have to adapt if they want to be as efficient as their competitors.

As the organizations adapt and grow, internal job specialization emerges because specialization is the most efficient way of getting things done. In a ten- person business operation, each worker can and often will do every job. That way, if one or two people call in sick, the others can pick up the slack. But in a five hundred or thousand person operation, it is inconceivable that everyone will be able to do every job.

Some contemporary businesses tried to keep a personal touch in their organizations despite the growth, but they couldn't do it, not to the extent they wanted. The loss of regular and direct employer-employee contact is one of the unfortunate costs of organizational success. When the small business operating out of a rented garage becomes a success, the owners move out of their cozy quarters, maybe into one floor of a commercial building. And they need more employees to handle the increased customer demands and to help create more demands so that they can hire even more people. You grow or you die is the credo of contemporary businesses. So the growth continues.

The growing company will eventually need a sales manager to monitor the development of the market, they will hire another MBA to oversee the daily production process and yet another to insure that the products are sent out in an efficient manner. They might need a legal department, and of course they will want a human resources expert. If and when the business really expands, the initial entrepreneurs might decide to go public so that they can cash out, buy a sail boat, and spend their days exploring mysterious tropical islands where people go naked in the sun. And meanwhile, a small and personal business operation becomes another symbol on the New York Stock Exchange. And yet another bureaucracy emerges.

People who start small businesses do not always plan to go in the direction of the New York Stock Exchange. If they thought carefully about it, they might even decide that they don't want to grow that much because the fun would go out of what they are doing. But if the growth and the success do come, and in the process they create yet another bureaucracy, that outcome is not necessarily bad or even unfortunate. It only illustrates that despite what people might want or what they might plan, bureaucracies are an inevitable outcome of organizational growth. Despite their reputations, they are the most efficient form of complex organization yet devised. If they were not, someone like Ben or Jerry would have come up with an alternative. They didn't. And as yet, no one else has.

Why are bureaucratic organizations so irritating despite being so efficient? You think that everyone would admire an efficient system for getting things done. Unfortunately, that efficiency comes at a price, and anyone who has ever worked in a bureaucratic organization or has tried to get some problem handled by that structure can attest.

Workers in bureaucratic settings are specialists. Employees have certain tasks, often very small tasks. But in time, usually a very short time, individuals learn to do their jobs very well. And when they are in an office with hundreds of other workers all doing their small jobs very well, the organization and its products operate with considerable efficiency even if all the jobs are somewhat tedious. That job tedium is one part of the price for bureaucratic efficiency. In this case, it is only the employees who pay.

If the organization is well managed, there will also be clear lines of responsibility and authority. Individuals know what they are supposed to do and they know what they are permitted to do under their specific and usually written job guidelines. Some years ago, when I worked in a telephone company business office, the service representatives who handled customer complaints were allowed to make adjustments on phone calls up to one dollar. Their supervisor had to approve any adjustment above a dollar, and the supervisors had to check with their bosses for any adjustment more than ten dollars.

This approval process may sound cumbersome, and it probably was to a customer calling with a complaint about a twenty-dollar call on their bill that they didn't make. But frustrating though it was for a few customers, and demeaning though the process was to the more experienced and capable service representatives, this process and a thousand other similar processes within bureaucratic organizations works because they are efficient most of the time. Employees develop skills in handling routine matters, and as long as the contacts are routine, the process is efficient. Customers who have unusual cases will probably run into some delay in resolving their complaints. Delays in handling the *unusual cases* are another cost factor of bureaucratic efficiency. And in this case, it is the customer who pays the charges.

Bureaucrats know that if they do their jobs well, if they don't abuse their areas of authority and responsibility, there is a good chance for career advancement, at least as long as the organization survives. This potential for advancement in both salary and responsibility is another characteristic that makes bureaucracies efficient. The organizations are meritocracies, where employees are promoted because of good job performance. Bureaucrats who do their jobs can be reasonably successful without worrying about the boss's son being brought in to take over a department. Although, as some authors argued, the motivation of only doing your job can lead to everyone in the organization rising to their level of incompetence, this unfortunate scenario is not necessarily the way bureaucracies should or do work.

Although bureaucracies are generally efficient then, there is potential for a down side to this efficiency. The job specialization can generate a pervasive tunnel vision in employees so they do not see much that goes on beyond the next desk or office pod. That specialization can also make it difficult for any organization to communicate a sense of its mission to workers.

If managers are not careful, that restricted vision can also lead to inertia in the organization. If employees get too comfortable, too complacent with what they are doing, they might not be responsive to procedural changes, even when the changes would be good for the organization. That kind of distorted perspective can easily infect an entire organization and the results could be fatal. Bureaucracies may be efficient, but they are not immortal.

So, like most people, bureaucracies have their good side and their bad side, their pluses and their minuses, their yings and their yangs. Properly managed, and this is admittedly no small chore, they are efficient, responsive, and creative organizations that do the job better than any alternative. Poorly managed, as they occasionally are, the organizations can be maddeningly unresponsive, slow to change, and unsympathetic to customer concerns. Poor, weak, or corrupt leadership can destroy any organization, however large or long its history, and we have seen recent examples of this destruction. On the flip side though, creative, energetic leadership can have the opposite effect and re-energize even a previously moribund organization.

The real problem with bureaucracies then is not so much with the organization itself as with their management. There are some potential problems when you create a large organization with thousands of specialists, each occupying one small niche in a large and complex working system. The trick is to maintain a sense of cohesion along with an awareness of mission and not incidentally, paying some attention to all the seemingly little things that support strong employee morale.

Everyone wants the bottom line, so here it is with bureaucracies. It is silly and frequently destructive to belittle the Washington bureaucrats, the educational bureaucracy, or any other bureaucratic organization operating within our modern industrial society. Bureaucracies are a part of our contemporary lives and until someone comes up with a more efficient organizational alternative, they are going to stay. We may not like their impersonality, the narrow and sometimes unfulfilling jobs, or the mind-numbing inertia in the daily organizational routine. Who would like such things? But there is no rule that says we have to accept the negative parts or resist changing them. We don't have to, as that old adage tells us, throw out the baby with the bath water.

We should remember that we do like the efficiency and the economies of scale that bureaucracies bring to our dinner tables, our garages, and our homes. As Ben and Jerry might say, even with a bureaucracy, you can still make some great ice cream.

CHAPTER 12

Was It Meant to Be?

● ● ●

Whosoever quarrels with his fate does not understand it!

BETTINE

ASK ANY GROUP OF TEN sociologists, if you can find that many in one grouping, what they consider the primary difficulties facing contemporary Americans and they will put *alienation* on their lengthy lists. Even if they aren't sure it belongs, they feel obligated to list it because alienation is one of the *loss leader* items in the sociology market. For people who have never worked in a retail outlet, a loss-leader is an item that you sell below cost in order to bring customers into the store.

Anyway, alienation is to sociologists what supply and demand are to economists or what anal and retentive are to psychologists. Take supply and demand away from economics and you destroy a thousand academic careers. Maybe more! And there is no way to get the anal retentive out of psychology (or out of the psychologists). So it is with alienation in sociology, a veritable *sine qua non*! Let me take a stab at explaining this slippery term. (alienation, not *sine qua non*!)

Contemporary Americans have access to conveniences that earlier generations would have drooled over. Even today, many global residents envy the American lifestyle. (What do they know?) But the components of our modern, presumably easier world, the PC's, the IPOD's, DVD's,

BVD's, PVC's. and BMWs, all the captivating gadgets may not be much comfort in an indifferent world.

The frantic pace of modern life, along with an impersonal and increasingly insecure work place, superficial or strained family relationships, and transient communities, the pressures can instill a feeling that the individual doesn't belong. He sees himself being alone, with the people in his life acting indifferent or even hostile to his needs. And if he sees himself that way, he is what sociologists call *alienated*. It is easy to see why sociologists are so attracted to the concept; it has a lot of *bells and whistles* to it.

In a silent film from several generations ago, Charlie Chaplin portrayed a helpless worker caught in an industrial gear. That classic silent film still has meaning. Workers who spent lifetimes in one organization, finishing their working lives with gold watches celebrating their longevity, are the exception now. Serial employment is the new social norm, where individuals change their jobs almost as often as they change their cars. Sometimes more often. Workers have no commitment to an employer; from professional ball players to computer geeks, individuals work for an organization only until something better comes along. The employees are, in turn, seen as digits on a computer printout by managers who crunch numbers, careers, and lives with about the same emotional involvement.

Neighborhoods are not much better as locations for connecting to another human being. Everyone seems to be either moving or planning to move and why bother making friends with the neighbors because you'll be moving soon. Other than a quick wave on the way to work, a short conversation, and maybe a glass of iced tea while working in the yard, neighbors don't connect as often.

Even families feel the effects of the hectic lifestyle. Family dinners at home are the exception. Every family member, even the kids, is too busy to sit down for a relaxed dinner. Outside agencies have emerged to take over many of the traditional family responsibilities. With this sense of disengagement from the family unit as well as work and home, it is not surprising that so many Americans feel detached from their lives and their worlds.

If my memory is correct, and it isn't always, the alienation, that sense of a hostile and unresponsive world, started for me when I was in kindergarten. It was just before the Christmas vacation, and the teacher planned a holiday grab bag for the students, an event designed to prevent bad feelings because of who spent how much on what gift. The economics in that school were decidedly mixed. A few of us came from families of relatively moderate means, households where, when new shoes were necessary, parents bought them several sizes too big so that the kids could "grow into them." Wedged between that decision and the parent's intention to wear the shoes "until they wore out," I concluded that I spent less than half of my childhood wearing shoes that actually fit.

Speaking of shoes, judging from the quality of my schoolmates' gym shoes, and that is as good an index of community economics as any other figure, most of the kids in that kindergarten class came from families with comfortable incomes. I had reason to expect a good return on my own grab-bag investment, a fire engine that was state-of-the-art in its day. The ladder went up and down, the wheels turned, and you could actually take the driver out of the truck, a feature that back then was what might now be called high tech.

I actually debated, as much as a five year old kid can be said to debate anything, the idea of keeping the fire engine and skipping the event. I could have called in sick that day and kept the truck. But that thought didn't last long because my mother refused to consider the idea; "We bought that toy for your school party, and that is where you are going to take it" were her final words in what passed for a debate.

And so, with mixed feelings, I put that fire truck with the movable ladder into the large cardboard box in the school room, where it rested alongside some thirty other gifts. I remember thinking that although I would not have the truck, I might come home with something better. Oh, the fantasies I had: an air rifle (they were the days before *zero tolerance*), a monopoly game, a silver cap gun with a leather holster, it was even possible that I could extract a Sears's gift certificate that could put me on a new bike. There was that kind of money floating around the community.

The teacher decided that class scholarship would determine the order for selecting gifts. In kindergarten, then as now, being a good student meant that you stood quietly while waiting for the bell to ring, you cut within the lines, and you did not put too much paste on your handicraft projects. By such standards, I was the class salutatorian. So when I dipped my hand into that cardboard gift box, all the good stuff was still there. The first kid got a set of Lincoln Logs. Not bad, but treasures were still there for the taking.

When I reached into the box, eyes closed as per instructions, I put my little hands not around something large, like a box, or a barrel, and I did not reach for something soft, since I was afraid of getting a stuffed animal or a doll, neither of which were on my wish list. I remember rummaging around long enough so that the teacher told me to "hurry up." The pressure was on! I must have panicked, because I somehow came up with a brown paper lunch bag, stapled at the top as though its contents could spill.

I had no reason to be disappointed. For all I knew, that little brown bag could hide that Sears gift certificate or even some ready cash put in the bag by a harried parent. Five dollars, for example, would have given me financial security for the rest of my life. Or so it seemed at the time. Thirty sets of eyes were on me as I opened the bag. What I extracted was not a gift certificate or even a five-dollar bill. It was a small red plastic helicopter about the size of an adult's index finger. So much for the notion that big things come in small packages.

What I saw was what I got; the helicopter had no secret compartments, nothing to wind, no removable pilot inside, and to add to my growing sense of despair, two of the four blades were missing. I felt like a victim of the "bait and switch" procedure; either that, or the Enron Corporation had been in charge of the gift process.

What could I do? It was too late to throw the damn thing back. I looked at the teacher, hoping for a reprieve, expecting to hear her say, "Would you like to pick something else?" No such luck. She smiled, although I'm sure she was thinking something along the lines of, "that poor schmuck."

My moment was over. Other, destined to be luckier, kids were waiting, and the teacher waved me to the sidelines like a basketball player who had fouled out of the game. I sat in silence, staring at the broken helicopter while the gift selections continued around me. Each new draw from the grab bag brought someone a new treasure, and each time I listened to the "ooh's" and "ahh's," I remember thinking, "That could have been me. That should have been me!"

When all the gifts had been distributed, the teacher gave us a play period so that we could share our new prizes. It will, I am sure, come as no surprise to learn that none of the kids wanted to play with the helicopter. My helicopter! Even I didn't want anything to do with it. I tried trading it for a coloring book, and even for one of the three stuffed animals that were in the box. No deals!

I watched from the sidelines as the rest of the class paraded around with their board games, erector sets, paint books, and of course, that red fire engine. Even Steven Spielberg would have had an imagination meltdown if he tried to work with that two-bladed helicopter. If this was the end of my personal frustrations, it wouldn't be much of a narrative about alienation. Kid wants a nice toy, kid doesn't get a nice toy, end of a story. Big deal! But the unfolding story of my alienation only started in that kindergarten room; I just didn't know it yet.

The next major episode, I will not burden the reader with the minor occurrences, happened a few short years later, while I was still immersed in my elementary school career. For some reason, the third graders presented a class play for the PTA, a three act, mercifully short portrayal about a group of young people who sit around someone's kitchen on the day before Thanksgiving lamenting the fact that they "had nothing to be thankful for." I had no trouble getting into the spirit of that play.

I also had one of the lead roles. If this had been the legitimate theater, my name would have been on the marquee. One of the significant early moments in the play, the equivalent maybe of the time when Juliet finds Romeo's seemingly lifeless body (or was it the other way around?), occurred when I picked up a nutcracker from the table in front of me, put a walnut in it, and was supposed to say to the audience after I cracked the shell; "I don't know what we have to be thankful for." (Ending sentences with a preposition is acceptable in the legitimate theater!) The sound of that nut cracking was the signal for a group of Pilgrims to walk onto the stage and lecture us spoiled kids about what a wonderful life we had. Like they knew!

The time was at hand. Up to that moment, and doubtlessly to the surprise of everyone trapped in that assembly hall, the performances had been flawless. Or as flawless as elementary school kids can be. And although it would be a stretch to describe them as "spellbound," the audience was reasonably attentive. Even the flash cameras were silent. It was time for the walnut moment.

When you think about the odds, it still seems unlikely, like holding the winning lottery ticket. Out of the millions of walnuts grown that year, and from the thousands available in local stores, our teacher had selected a mutant, a nut so hard that it could have served as a ball bearing. (This is what the teacher said afterwards.)

But I am getting ahead of my story. There I was, sitting on the stage, wearing new clothes, a fresh haircut, I had my little hands around a metal nutcracker, and I was trying to crush this iron ball disguised as a walnut. Even at the age of eight, I broke into a rolling sweat. In my mind's eye, sheets of water were gathering on the table and were about to wash over the stage. A Niagara Falls of perspiration, disgusting the entire front row and embarrassing my parents forever. But there was nothing to be done. I couldn't run screaming from the stage, although the thought did enter my mind. All I could do was to keep trying to crack that nut.

The audience was reasonably sympathetic. At least they didn't throw anything. They did start to laugh though, once they figured out what was happening. In the beginning, the laughter was slow, like the first uncomfortable titters in an off-color night club act. After a few minutes though, the place erupted. A sensitive play about the American dream turned into a Chevy Chase comedy; Fletch Makes Walnut Dressing!

Most of the people sitting out there were probably thankful it wasn't their kid on the stage. From what I was told later, my father pulled a Simon Peter, insisting to everyone around him that he had no idea who the kid was. After a period of time that I remember as unnecessarily excessive, the teacher sent the pilgrims on stage. The script resumed, but neither the play nor I ever recovered. At the end of the play, we were supposed to have another emotional scene, when I picked up yet another walnut, cracked it, and announced; "Well, now I know what we should be thankful for!" It is not hard to imagine what happened then, during what otherwise might have been a theatrical moment on a par with Humphrey Bogart saying "here's looking at you, kid" to a tearful Ingrid Bergman.

High school also had its helicopter moments, as I started calling them, more evidence, as if I were looking for it, which I wasn't, that there was some sort of celestial bulls eye painted on my back. I was beginning to think there might be such a thing as fate. There had to be some reason for what was going on around me. This couldn't be pure chance!

Anyway, it was with understandable apprehension that I found myself on the high school auditorium stage in the second half of my freshman year, standing in front of more than four hundred teenagers whose social sensitivity scores were on the low end of any distribution curve. What produced this situation was a concert by the high school's Beginning Band students and what led to this concert is a vital part of this sad episode.

Like most adolescent males, I did not like the idea of standing in front of a group. And when you were going to be standing or singing in front of your peers, it was difficult to imagine anything worse. But every freshman student enrolling in first year music class had to go through this humiliating procedure. There were no exceptions. Even the guy with the stuttering problem had to sing a song in his freshman music class. But that is another story.

The only legitimate escape from the songfest was to take band class. Normally (at least this was the conventional wisdom handed down by my older brother), band was a breeze. You pretended to be interested in some instrument and your lack of either talent or motivation was lost in a sea of kids with similar inclinations. The charade only lasted for a year, until the two required semesters of music education were completed. And you didn't have to sing!

But as I was slowly beginning to discover, things rarely went "normally" for me. The year I came to high school, the kindly band director who had been at the school for generations went on a sabbatical. He had never taken a sabbatical before, and from what I heard, he never took one again. But he was on leave my freshman year, and his replacement was a musical zealot.

This fanatic, there is no other word to describe him, decided that it would be fun (his word!) to have a school concert. Trying his best to justify his notion of fun to us, he explained that the concert would show everyone how well the new band members were doing and would also, and here he demonstrated a glaring ignorance about the students in his Beginning Band class, provide us with a special advantage when we applied for senior band. As if such an application had entered any of our minds.

No one that I knew was interested in this special advantage. Most of us had no intentions of coming to that band room any longer than the rules required. But we were trapped. If there was anything good about the situation, it was that we couldn't all play solos. My peers and I could only hope that some other poor slobs would get picked. The selection day came, and no one stayed home; there was more chance to plead your case if you were there in person. As I remember, at least three of the band students limped into class that morning, claiming serious injuries from strenuous weekend activities. They were the smart ones.

It was no surprise when the director pointed to me and said, "of course you'll have to play a solo." Naturally I had to play a solo, because I was the solitary tenor sax player (it was the only instrument left when it was my turn to pick!). I was trapped! I had played that unwieldy instrument for approximately seven weeks and the nearest thing to a lesson I had was when the band director walked by the saxophone section and told me,

"Try not to blow so hard." Mr. Holland he was not. And since my music reading ability never extended beyond the key of C, most of the time I only pretended to play, relying on my peers to make enough noise so that no one would notice the absence, or alternatively the bad notes, coming from the tenor sax.

For the benefit of readers without a background in band instruments, the tenor sax, besides being large and loud, with a noise something like a bull moose in heat, is a reed instrument. The musician, in this case, me, uses a removable mouthpiece when blowing into the device. The mouthpiece has a replaceable flat bamboo insertion about the size of an emery board, for people familiar with such things. If you want to play the saxophone and have it sound good, or as good as a sound is going to get in the hands and mouth of an amateur, the bamboo reed has to be in perfect condition; no cracks, no chips, no breaks. To minimize the potential for any problems that would come from a cracked reed, I purchased one especially for the performance.

Remember now, this musical solo, by definition, was going to be just me. There would be no pretending to blow, no trumpets, clarinets, or drums covering for me as we stumbled our way through pieces such as *Yankee Doodle Dandy.* I had to get through this solo or I was going to be the first student in the school's history to flunk Beginning Band. Worse that that, failure meant that I would be singing in front of some music class. The alternatives were unacceptable; the solo had to happen!

But I had a plan. I selected a short version of "Home Sweet Home," in the key of C of course, and thus posing few opportunities for error. I rehearsed as much as I could, considering the fact that not only did I hate the instrument, but it was too heavy to consider hauling it the mile or so and back and forth from my house. But two stanzas of Home Sweet Home, thirty or forty notes, no sharps, no flats, just enough for everyone to know what the song was, or what it was supposed to be, and I was done. I didn't expect and didn't want any audience sing-along.

I had a brand new reed still in the wrapper and I was not going to remove the wrapper until just before the concert. I was, in other words, as prepared as it was possible to be. Unfortunately, I did not look up. If I had, I would have seen the helicopter circling and the pilot pointing at me and laughing while he trained his guns on my back.

I stood behind the heavy red velvet curtain on the stage, opened my reed and started moistening it in a mouth that was dry with fear. One by one, my peers trudged on stage and, even to my untrained ear, they sounded awful. True music lovers, if there were any in that audience, would have been in tears. I'm going to fit right in with this parade, I thought, and my confidence level took a sharp upward turn. I even allowed myself a smile. Hell, I might even be good by the standards out there.

Then I heard the sound of a trumpet. Not your typical, beginning-band, trumpet, but something like the sound that might have occurred if Louis Armstrong had stopped by for a short gig. As it turned out, my predecessor on that stage was good old Sidney Stahl. Sid was a nice enough guy, but he did not belong in Beginning Band. Sid started playing the trumpet right after he started to walk and not incidentally, he went directly into senior band two weeks after that concert, something that had never happened before. And did not happened again, at least not while I was in high school.

But I was talking about his piece on the stage. Sid's rendition of, "When the Saints go Marching In," had the audience stamping their feet. The kids loved old Sid, and he took three bows, the last one with the zealot himself. The audience was still buzzing about the performance when it was my turn to walk through the red curtain. I walked out onto that stage and nodded to old Sid on his way back through the curtain. I think I may have glared at him. Then I looked out over that sea of faces and saw the audience look at me with the same kind of expectation they would have had if Jerry Seinfeld had just finished a monologue. They were expecting more high quality entertainment.

Is it necessary to say that they didn't get it? The experience was going to be even worse that I imagined it could be. As soon as I blew the first note, or what passed for a note, the ear-piercing squeal announced the news to the listening world. Impossible, my mind told my mouth, this brand new reed can't be cracked! Such things don't happen! But it had happened. And I had no choice but to continue. There was no place to run.

"Home Sweet Home" sounded as though I was dragging a baseball cleat across the length of a blackboard. Although it was no more than forty notes and just one or two minutes long, it seemed an eternity. When I took a moment to glance up from my music, I saw the audience pointing, poking their neighbors, and whipping one another into a psychological frenzy. Everyone, students, teachers, even that damn band director, was laughing. I knew how Hester Prynne must have felt when she stood on the platform facing such rampant hostility and realizing that she would be wearing a scarlet letter for a long, long time.

Fortunately, after what seemed about nine years, my high school career ended. But my fate was apparently right on track. And alienation was growing faster than anyone would have predicted. As time passed, even routine events took unexpected, even bizarre turns when I came on the scene. Cash registers froze up, computers crashed, cars didn't start, even at a young age, I began to feel like that cartoon character who walks around with a storm cloud over his head.

College provided no relief. When I showed up for registration that first semester, the only physical education class left was boxing. No one ever wanted to take boxing class. It was filled with either individuals like me, who were trapped, or sociopaths who enjoyed beating the crap out of someone. During that first semester, I started each day with my boxing class; I got the crap beat out of me, and then tried to focus on the writings of Descartes in my Philosophy class. It was not a productive sequence.

After two years of college, I joined the armed services, hoping to find some direction in my life and maybe outrun my destiny. It wasn't even a close race. The drill instructor assigned to my platoon had been ready to retire. He would have made a great mercenary in one of the foreign wars, and maybe that is where he was going, but "fortunately," (the word used by the company commander when he addressed us prior to the start of basic training) the Army convinced Sgt. Lee to train "just one more group of recruits."

Clint Eastwood would have walked across the street to avoid running into this guy. Sergeant Lee made John Wayne's Sergeant Striker look like Mohandas Ghandi. Lee never smiled, and he was strong and mean enough to rip a full field pack off your back if you got out of step during a march. I speak from personal experience. And this man was my drill instructor. As soon as I glanced at that face, I silently swore to stay out of the man's path. But despite my vow of anonymity, or probably because of it, we got acquainted very quickly.

Back then, the army distributed rifles to the recruits during the second week of basic training. We were told to oil our instruments of death quickly because the enemy could come at any time. The supply clerk also warned us to be sure that the rifle had everything it was supposed to have because the weapon was our means of survival. More than that, the rifle was our personal responsibility. If we didn't return all the equipment including the rifle in perfect shape at the end of our training cycle, we would have to do basic training again. That was more than enough incentive.

Even as someone handed it to me and I read the serial number to the supply clerk, I sensed that this would not be a "normal" rifle. I only hoped that the deficiency, whatever it was, could be ignored, or that the problem would be simple, like a missing strap or a slightly bent front sight. I could always correct such things later. Quietly.

But the instrument would not work without the bolt that held the firing pin. If the gun wouldn't send bullets out, I might as well have turned it into a planter. And there would be no way to fake it at the firing range unless I found a way to throw the bullets at the target with enough speed. There was no choice. I had to walk up to my drill instructor and tell him that there was something wrong with my gun.

What followed was my first hard-won lesson in the army, that you don't use the word "gun," especially not in front of a drill instructor. What they have given to you to defend the American way of life is a rifle not a gun. If the U.S. Army was a religion, then making the mistake of calling a rifle a gun would be cause for excommunication. Actually, I would have preferred excommunication or almost any form of physical torture other than gouging out of eyes. I have never liked the idea of anyone fooling around with my eyes. The humiliation handed out to me on that morning was thorough, efficient, and totally demoralizing. I was about to become all I could be, and I could tell right away that it was not going to be a fun experience.

There are other stories, but I did promise only one more. The point anyway is not a series of sad experiences but how a sense of alienation from society might develop in a person. Once you begin to feel as though the world is not on your side, or even that the world is against you, it seems sensible to get as far away from it as you can.

Alienation is not a fatal condition. You could define it as just another means of adjustment. Why get involved with a cold, cruel, and uncaring world? Alienation is neither good nor bad, just another way of adjusting. The problems emerge when and if the alienated individual elects to strike out at the unresponsive world. Various political and religious groups have tapped into this well of individual frustration, and this changes alienation from a personal to a social problem.

I sometimes wonder, especially after I have a few beers, about the kid who brought the helicopter to school that day. Who was she? What was on her mind, or on her mother's mind, with that gift? Was it intent or haste, or even fate that prompted them to put a broken helicopter into that lunch bag on party day?

Maybe the astrologers are right, that there is a plan, a fate that directs our lives and all we can do is to go with the flow. Would my life have taken different turns if I had picked one of the stuffed animals from the grab bag? At this point, who knows!

And who cares!

CHAPTER 13

You Can't Stop Progress?

● ● ●

MODERN LIFE IS FAST AND the frantic pace can be brutal. Sometimes, and understandably, a few people lose interest in trying to keep up.

Whenever construction starts on another new shopping mall, or workers begin carving out another highway extension connecting older highway extensions, or we watch a new cluster of homes surrounded by freshly planted hedges replacing what use to be a stand of oak trees, someone will remind the people in the path of that change and destruction and the rest of us reading about it that *progress is inevitable. More than that, they might say,* progress is desirable, a social anchor in the cultural sea, if that metaphor makes any sense.

Americans hear about this progress enough that the announcements begin to sound like the recording you hear when you call the cable company and a recorded voice insists "your call is important to us!" I would not be surprised to discover that somewhere in the labyrinth of state and federal government offices, there was an Under Secretary for Progress. In the federal branch, the office might be in the Interior Department, although the position could have been transferred to the new Department of Homeland Security because what could be more central to homeland security than progress?

The vital task of this progress office would be to insure that all Americans, or most of them, understand the value of progress. If a few unpatriotic Luddites did not appreciate the contributions made by progress, the Under Secretary could take steps to insure that the malcontents never mounted any effective opposition.

Fortunately for our governmental representatives, the country doesn't need this hypothetical Under Secretary for Progress because there is so little effective opposition. Groups and individuals arguing against progress get the same reception from their fellow Americans as the Hare Krishna's walking the nation's airports, or the lonely people who walk around federal buildings with their hand-made signs extolling the virtues of free speech. Who has time to worry about free speech?

The important people have managed to turn progress into one of the country's basic values, right there alongside truth, justice, profits, and the American way. But it is useful to look at our basic values once in awhile and ask a few questions, just to see if everyone is comfortable with what is going on under this appealing values rubric. Progress, for example, sounds good. Who wants their name on a list of people opposed to progress?

What would you be stopping if you blocked progress, if in fact you managed to, which you probably couldn't even if you wanted to? Would that act make you a contemporary Luddite, a pathetic person living in the past and opposed to change because it makes you uncomfortable? Or because you lost your job? Get over it, someone will tell you, because if we don't have progress, that leaves us with *stagnation* as the only option.

Some interesting questions and claims, but before tackling them, we should define the term that everyone, including me, is throwing about with reckless abandon. Exactly what is progress? Is it always good? And is it inevitable in modern society?

Despite its common use, or maybe because of it, there is little precision associated with the term *progress*. We can use the dictionary, but there isn't much help in its pages. Webster, who does well with so many words, defines progress as, *to improve, to advance toward perfection.*

Progress is appealing when described like this; how could improvement or moving toward perfection be anything but a good thing? But exactly what did the dictionary writers mean by *improve*? How precise is that? How do we measure *advancement*, and not incidentally, what is *perfection?* We started with one vague term, and now we have three. We do not seem to be making much progress.

It might be more productive to use a different approach, one immortalized by Justice Potter Stewart's definition of pornography. I am not suggesting that progress is the same as pornography, although it could lead to some interesting discussions. Anyway, in a decision that is now of interest only to historians and perhaps Justice Stewart's descendants, he wrote that pornography was something he couldn't define but he would know it when he saw it.

If we apply that subjective explanation to the notion of progress, if, for example, Justice Stewart examined the prospect of developers carving out a six-lane highway through pristine forests, he might not be able to define it, but he presumably would know whether the resulting landscape change constituted progress. He would know progress when he saw it.

Unfortunately what might have worked for pornography won't help much with progress. We need a measure that will provide better guidelines. For one thing, it would be useful to know if, and then how much, or how little, progress there was.

Let us suppose that developers selected a tranquil wetlands area as a locale for a new housing cluster; developers are drawn to wetlands areas in a fashion not unlike iron filings toward a magnet. The developers will argue that the proposed activity constitutes progress for the entire region.

The progress is obvious, they will say; we are building new homes in what once was a hazardous swamp filled with mosquitoes, thousands of unhealthy crawling bugs, and strange plants that are unhealthy for children and pets. Their glossy brochures will include snapshots of attractive children playing with Golden Retriever puppies on acres of weed-free lawns.

Who would not prefer a sea of green lawns and sculptured flower gardens to fallen and rotting trees, standing water, and swarms of biting insects that attack our children and their pets? But we have to look beyond that appealing picture to get a more accurate idea of what happens with all the new homes. We want to know whether the homes constitute an *improvement*.

Improvement is easier to handle than progress because improvement implies that the situation is better than it was. Assessing whether something is better should be less controversial than the vague idea of progress. Individuals who lose weight, for example, usually improve their health. And a machine that runs on less fuel is an improvement over a gas-guzzler. In physics at least, efficiency is always an improvement over inefficiency.

There is also an aesthetic component to the notion of improvement. Getting rid of junk cars on the city streets is a clear improvement in community appearance. Similarly, painted homes, depending on the choice of color, are an improvement over unpainted structures. And on the individual level, it would be fair to say that a homeless man with tattered clothing who had a bath, shave, haircut and new clothes, improved his appearance, perhaps to the point where he could run for public office.

But while we might be able to agree on the admittedly obvious examples of improvement, the term loses whatever clarity it has when we apply it to this hypothetical housing development. Let us put the developers and their brochures on a shelf for the moment.

From an environmental perspective, it would be impossible to *improve* a wetlands area. Wetlands provide habitat to a large variety of species, and although not all of the species are the cuddly type, they all, including the crawling and biting creatures, contribute to the overall health and stability of the ecological system. Every element in this system is not appealing to humans, but the various species have their respective niches. And if you keep eliminating unappealing species and their jobs, the whole structure eventually collapses. It is important to remember that the ecological structure collapses on everyone, not just on the snakes and spiders.

Humans and developers often forget, or chose to forget, that wetlands make a significant contribution to human welfare. Besides being home for numerous species, wetlands act as a sponge, a natural cleaning and filtering agent for area watersheds. Wetlands clean the water before it goes back into circulation. Take the sponges out of the system and what is going to do this cleaning? The answer, unfortunately, is nothing. A significant part of the nation's water problems stem from the elimination of its wetlands, or what we once called swamps.

Filling in wetlands to build housing might be an improvement to the families who will live in the homes, and it will improve the bottom lines of the businesses that sell lawn chemicals and other supplies to the new residents, but there are other individuals involved in this situation who have equally compelling interests. Besides the homeowners and businesses, individuals in the surrounding communities have a stake in that proposed housing development. Their voices are not often heard because even they may not understand how they are going to be affected. The problem is that the effects of this kind oif progress are often in*direct*.

Now what does that mean, "indirect?" Maybe a better description than indirect would be *not as obvious*. The *not so obvious effects* on other people's lives include poorer water quality for an entire region because of the loss of the wetlands and its cleaning capabilities. There could be significantly lower rainfall in other parts of the country because the wetlands will no longer feed moisture into the atmosphere. So we are talking about a potentially large effect on regional water quality and circulation. The affected group constitutes enough potential victims to get a gaggle of trial lawyers excited.

The species loss from wetlands destruction could start a chain effect that would drastically affect the local and regional ecosystems. The loss of a critical nesting site would affect not only the nesting species, but also other animals that may rely on the species as a food supply, and who in turn are food sources for yet other species. And any or all of the various species may provide critical roles in seed distribution, pollination, and pest control. It is a classic domino effect; filling in large wetlands in Illinois then could easily have repercussions as far south as Alabama and north to Canada. The problem is that we don't usually think about such things. When was the last time citizens from Alabama or Canada appeared at a zoning hearing in Illinois? Even the idea of such a prospect would be enough to give developers and their bankers nightmares.

But it is logical that the local interests of developers and businesses should be balanced against the concerns and interests of hundreds of thousands, even millions, of other people living downstream whose lives may be affected by the wetlands destruction. If we insisted on evaluating the value of a construction project only as part of a broader network of interests, which of course we never do, but if we did, it would be far more difficult to describe a new housing development constructed on local wetlands as an improvement.

New highways are used as signs of local improvement even more often than new houses, especially by incumbent politicians who love to cut the colorful ribbons opening new stretches of road. This notion of improvement stems from providing constituents the ability to drive from point A to point B without the inconvenience of slowing down at intersections or being forced to come to occasional stops. Presumably this represents a significant improvement in people's lives; thus the presumed progress.

To be fair, a new road would constitute an improvement in the lives of the construction people who work on the project. Working is certainly an improvement over not working. The project would also improve the economic well being of the people fortunate enough to own the land the government needed for the road; and I am always intrigued how often it is that politicians have some ownership in the land where roads are built. But that could be a subject for another time.

Of course we have to mention the bottom lines of the businesses that will congregate along the new roadways. Finally, and I suppose not incidentally, there are the individuals who will drive on that new road and get wherever it is that they are going faster, for a few weeks at least, until other drivers discover the time advantage which will then evaporate for everyone, leading to more traffic problems which will raise the call for yet another road, all in the name of progress.

Road builders and traffic reporters often refer to urban highways as arteries, presumably because the roads represent the region's vital conduits. It might be more appropriate to describe the roads as feeding tubes, the ones hospitals put into people who cannot take nourishment on their own. Overall though, the list of road construction beneficiaries is lengthy and it always includes a few wealthy and influential people. Or is that redundant!

What about the people without influence? What kinds of changes are coming for them? What improvements will the general community get from a new road? A different way of asking the question might be, what would happen in the community if the roads were not built?

Let's try to be reasonably objective and completely thorough. If they did not build the new highway, drivers would still get to where they had to go because they have no choice. Like worker ants with an obstacle in their path, they will find alternative routes to their destinations. They will crawl over obstacles it if they have to; fortunately many of them have four-wheel drive vehicles purchased with such a scenario in mind.

If the traffic jams get bad enough, workers might consider other options, such as finding a job closer to home, or finding a home closer to the job. Either choice would produce less driving, less carbon emissions, and arguably an improvement in the broader community's life.

Local industries might insist they would have problems finding enough workers if there were not convenient access roads. Someone ought to suggest that the companies consider re-locating to urban areas where the roads are already in place and ready for more cars. Older cities contain a host of abandoned commercial properties that, with a little TLC, could be ideal locations for a variety of commercial and industrial activities. And not incidentally, many of the same cities have mass transportation systems that would eliminate the automobile traffic problems. Everyone would be happy. Well, almost everyone.

At this point, we could reasonably conclude that not building the road constituted a surprisingly amount of improvement. A few readers, maybe more than a few, are screaming now about the unfairness of the simplistic and naïve illustrations used in the preceding discussions. Of course the examples were naïve and simplistic, but no more so than the examples developers and politicians use to emphasize *improvements* produced by new highway construction, new housing tracts, or any of a hundred other building projects.

Whenever anyone speaks about progress, it is useful to remember that the term can be a smokescreen to obscure the presence of self-interest. Samuel Johnson once said that patriotism is the last refuge of a scoundrel. He said a lot of provocative things, and if you haven't checked him out, you should. Anyway, borrowing from Dr. Johnson, it would not be unreasonable to say that the notion of progress is the last refuge of a developer.

When city residents oppose the construction of a new high rise building, their objections are not anti-progress; the objections probably stem from an opposition to more traffic congestion, less parking, more noise, and more demands on community services. The people are not standing in the way of *progress*; they are fighting reductions in the quality of their lives. When rural residents protest a new highway going through their farmland, they are not standing in the way of *improvement*; they are only trying to maintain their way of life.

If progress, or what we call progress, means a reduction in people's quality of life or the destruction of other ways of life, maybe we should find another term to describe what we are doing. I am suggesting that any definition of progress that does not consider the quality of people's lives, and *people* in this context means everyone who might be affected by a construction project, is missing an essential component.

One of General Electric's early corporate slogans was, *progress is our most important product.* Even though GE probably had something else on their collective corporate mind, the statement might be something most Americans could embrace if they agreed about what progress was, and especially what it was not.

After all, who would oppose advancement toward perfection?

CHAPTER 14

The Wrap.

● ● ●

It's like it ain't so much what a fellow does, but it's the way
the majority of folks is looking at him when he does it.

WILLIAM FAULKNER, As I LAY DYING

Now THAT WE ARE FINISHING this brief look at selected social issues, a few readers might be objecting to the omissions. You talked about issues like bureaucracy and alienation, but what about education, they would yell, if they are in a location that allows yelling, which is pretty much everywhere. Yelling is often a substitute for clear thought and it is used far more than it should be. Anyway, what about crime, someone else will yell, probably at the person who was yelling about education. Someone else is sure to ask, why didn't I mention domestic violence or terrorism? And what about pornography? Surely pornography is a major problem that deserves a chapter in this book.

In my defense, and I do have one, there are reasons for wrapping up the discussion even though there are social issues I have not discussed. First, and probably foremost, it would be difficult to go through every social issue plaguing contemporary America. If I had a series of town hall meetings, sessions that, by the way, are overrated in terms of their utility, and listened to all the comments and suggestions, I could compile a list of hundreds, even thousands of situations that someone would define as a problem.

I remember a recent discussion with a friend, a real cat lover, and she could not imagine any issue more pressing than the feral cats which were, in her words, "over-running the community." She was devoted to the task of rounding up the cats, and if you have never tried this, you have no idea of how difficult it can be. After she had a few cats crated, she carried them to a local vet, had them neutered, and then released them back into the neighborhood where at least they would not be producing any more feral cats. Although I doubt whether the birds were happy to see the cats coming back.

My friend was sincere in her devotion to what she saw as a major problem and while I could see her point, it was not the kind of situation that would get me to carry a sign. Actually there are not many social issues that would have me carrying a sign. I don't ever remember reading or hearing about any social issue or policy dispute where people carrying signs had a significant influence. There might have been a situation somewhere, at some time, when sign-carriers influenced social policy, but I can't recall one.

And this leads to the next point in my defense of the book's contents, that any listing of social issues is necessarily subjective. One person's emotional definition of a serious problem might be seen by others as no big deal. A lot of Americans see it as a problem, for example, that virtually anyone can purchase an automatic weapon. On the other side, a sizable proportion of citizens regard automatic weapons possession as an inalienable right guaranteed both by the 2nd amendment and God. Who would venture into the woods hunting aggressive deer without an automatic weapon on their shoulder? And who would not want an automatic weapon in the house if and when the front door is broken down by a herd of religious fanatics? Who indeed. Both sides have been known to walk around with signs.

Finally, a number of social issues, education and crime are two examples, have been studied pretty exhaustively. Amazon shows 35,472 results when you search for books on crime. And for education, there are 186,175 listings. I don't believe I have anything new to add to the already lengthy publication lists.

Despite the brief discussions here, or maybe because of them, there are some interesting inferences. One is, of course, the subjective nature of defining a problem. I mentioned this notion several times but it bears repeating. Repetition is an effective learning device.

Another conclusion is that although *common sense* might argue otherwise, there is nothing in any type of behavior that makes it a social problem. Even violence, something that is so obviously undesirable that, like malaria, you want to do everything you can to eradicate it, to stamp it out so that it never comes back - even violence is not always defined as a major problem.

American society has had a high rate of violence almost from its inception. Some scholars have argued that we have a culture of violence in this country. It is only at certain times, usually during political campaigns, that the rate of violence is defined as unacceptable or contrary to our basic values. And not incidentally, if you think there is disagreement over what a social problem is, try reaching a consensus about what constitutes our country's basic *values*.

And once the political campaigns are over, things go back to what most people define as normal. Unless they are affected directly, Americans are immune to the violence that permeates their world. "Ten murders in Chicago last week? And more than 16,000 in the country last year? Well, what can you do?" In an election year, the idea of sixteen thousand homicides a year might be seen as an unacceptable blemish. When the elections are over, the homicides are no longer a blemish.

When John Kennedy campaigned for president, he used the notion of a "missile gap" in his speeches, a notion that later analysis showed never existed. But the idea of this gap was a convenient political tool that Kennedy used quite effectively. Whether or not there was an actual gap was incidental. If enough people said it and enough people believed it, then there was a gap.

We are struggling through another political campaign this year, and among other slogans, there is the promise to "make America great again." There are also lots of promised commitments to "rebuild our military." If

I were sitting across from any of the candidates, and I can't say it would be something I would love doing, but if I were, I would be asking them, when were we ever weak? Right now, we spend more on weapons than the next eight countries combined. We have enough explosives many times over to get rid of everyone walking the planet. We don't need to wonder when can we make America great again; we need to ask, how much is enough?

But again, if someone says there is a problem, and enough people believe her, then it becomes a problem. Understanding that fundamental principle takes us a long way in understanding social issues in America. My friend with the feral cats is not a significant person in the country, or even in her community. But if she were a senator or a presidential candidate, then her pronouncements about the cats would have a lot more weight. And you would see government trucks with uniformed drivers going around looking for stray cats.

Whatever the problems, real or imagined, there are rarely easy solutions. One solution is to declare the problem as solved and move on to other things. It's the flip side of defining something as a problem. Only here, you are taking an existing problem and telling everyone, "Stop worrying, this is no longer a problem!" A few individuals have suggested this as the best way to deal with the nation's drug problem. And that process is almost guaranteed to work. Remember, if no one sees a situation as a problem, then it is not a problem. The idea seems deceptively simple; and it is. Ask George Orwell.

More money is always helpful, and sometimes essential, in dealing with social issues. But it is rarely the only solution. Or even the most important. In 2010, Mark Zuckerberg donated 100 million dollars of his hard-earned money to the Newark, New Jersey school system, thinking that the financial infusion would help to turn the failing school system around. The generous donation apparently didn't turn anything around other than the bank accounts of a few consultants. According to some reports, the money made things worse.

Sometimes we go after the wrong problems because of bad data or misinterpretation of good data. . Low scores on standardized exams, for example, might indicate a problem with the exams rather than with the schools. There is a general affection for numbers and their apparent precision, but that affection can be misplaced. I can't remember how many times I was surprised when a marginal student in one of my classes bragged about his "high GPA," or when a student who seemed incredibly bright told me that she "had only a 2.3 average."

When I worked for the telephone company, and as part of a university class I was taking on testing, I looked at the employment exams the telephone company used. I found no correlation between the test scores and job performance. Indeed, the people who only "marginally passed" turned out to be the best performing employees. I sent my analysis to the appropriate company officials, but nothing happened. When I asked about my analysis, the explanation was, "Yes, it was interesting, but we have used this test for a long time."

And finally, as discussed in earlier chapters, many parts of our society are changing. The changes include alterations in cultural values, technology, marital practices, and community stability, and all of them affect what we as a society define as problems and what we are willing and able to do about them. Maybe change itself is the foundation of our problems. Maybe we should do away with the changes.

Each time I look at what happens with social issues, the infusion of money or the absence of it, the policies designed for ideological reasons rather than sound information, and the persistent tendency in American society to attempt, again and again, to legislate some long ago morality, I am amazed and disappointed at how little progress we have made over the past few generations. I conducted classes on social issues for more than twenty years, and at the end of my teaching career, I was still talking about most of the same things.

I guess that Abraham Lincoln said it best; it hurts too much to laugh, but I'm too big to cry.

www.ingramcontent.com/pod-product-compliance
Lightning Source LLC
Chambersburg PA
CBHW072127280526
45788CB00002B/572